Counselling skills
FOR CHURCH
COMMUNITY WORKERS

Counselling skills
FOR CHURCH AND FAITH
COMMUNITY WORKERS

Alistair Ross

Open University Press
Maidenhead · Philadelphia

Open University Press
McGraw-Hill Education
McGraw-Hill House
Shoppenhangers Road
Maidenhead
Berkshire
England
SL6 2QL

email: enquiries@openup.co.uk
world wide web: www.openup.co.uk

and
325 Chestnut Street
Philadelphia, PA 19106, USA

First Published 2003

A catalogue record of this book is available from the British Library

ISBN 0 335 20055 9 (pb)   0 335 20056 7 (hb)

Library of Congress Cataloging-in-Publication Data
Ross, Alistair, 1957–
    Counselling skills for church and faith community workers / Alistair Ross.
        p.   cm.
    Includes bibliographical references (p.   ) and index.
    ISBN 0–335–20056–7 – ISBN 0–335–20055–9 (pbk.)
    1. Pastoral counseling.   2. Pastoral care.   I. Title.
    BV4012.2. R675   2003
    253.5 – dc21   2002042577

Typeset by RefineCatch Limited, Bungay, Suffolk
Printed in Great Britain by Bell and Bain Ltd, Glasgow

Contents

Preface and acknowledgements

Writing a book that can be accessible for members of different faith communities has been a challenging and enriching experience. The faith communities that find most expression in this book are Christianity (my own tradition) and Judaism – with their rich and long pastoral heritage (Oden 1984). The popular idea that choosing a religion is the same as picking up a favourite brand of breakfast cereal from the many on offer on a supermarket shelf is misguided. It fails to give recognition to the richness and diversity of what it is to be fully human and fully spiritual. This all-enveloping pluralism where everything is accorded an equal value and voice, and which dominates much of society, can rob or devalue specific religious traditions from contributing something of their distinctive development (Sacks 1995: 113–24). The pastoral traditions of the church or synagogue have something vitally important to say to all people, religious or not.

This book has been written for helpers or carers who either want to develop counselling skills or have wanted a framework for using the counselling skills they have already acquired. The illustrations come from real-life situations that I and other pastoral carers and counsellors have experienced. This diverse group of carers – male and female, faith leaders and lay workers, multi-denominational and multi-faith, ethnically diverse – has enriched and added texture and colour to the numerous pastoral situations described. In the interests of confidentiality the majority of names in this book have been changed, although some people wanted to retain their own. In a few cases I have also changed the gender and sometimes built a composite character based on several people experiencing the same issue. All the situations mentioned are real and likely to be encountered among the vast range of people's pastoral experiences.

Many of the quotations have been drawn from the counselling, psychotherapy and psychoanalytic literature. So words like 'client' and 'patient' are used to describe the real person-to-person human encounters that are at the heart of all good pastoral work. The illustrations shed light on this vitally important pastoral task in faith communities.

There are a large number of thanks to be made to people who have helped shape me and my pastoral work, a story that is found elsewhere in *Evangelicals in Exile* (Ross 1997). Special thanks go to Michael Jacobs for his long-suffering patience and skill as an editor; Moira Walker for her training of my infant psychodynamic skills; Sue Wheeler for her supportive supervision; Angela Hetherington as a fellow author and friend; Pat Bradley for her wrestling with my English; Margaret Hopkinson, Malcolm Goodspeed, Joan Whyman; and to Esther and Fishel Cohen for their gentle and encouraging comments about my growing understanding of Judaism. Writing this book has coincided with the establishment of the Institute of Pastoral Counselling (www.pastoral-counselling.co.uk) by my good friends and colleagues Ruth Layzell, Philip Allin and Rosemary Langford-Bellaby. An ongoing support has been the Planning Group and attendees of the Continuing the Journey Conference over the last decade, especially Tim Marks. Singular thanks also go to Mike Ellis, the source of most of my book collection and a long-standing friend who will write his own book some day. Other thanks are due to friends who have stood by me when life was far from easy and some of the pressures of being a pastoral carer weighed heavily: Andy Sparkes, Paul Goodliff, Geof Colmer, Geoff and Mary, Eileen and Owen, Ivan and Marilyn; and to Wendy Robinson for being such an insightful therapist and support. Special mention goes to Liz, my twin, for being there from the start; Ruth for sharing so much of this journey; and to Judy, my lovely wife, who has done all the DIY, gardening, decorating and much more besides to let me have time to do this book. Hannah and Toby have been supportive in their unique ways: Hannah for buying me two volumes on Freud from her monthly allowance; and Toby for making me play snooker and think about other things.

Alistair Ross

Chapter 1

Carers not counsellors

Linda was the head teacher of a demanding inner city primary school in London. As a new minister in the area I had gone in to see her to ask if I could do an assembly and she explained to me the local education authority's policy about multi-faith recognition and how she didn't want to 'push' a particular religion. I did point out that in an effort to be politically correct she was discriminating against Christianity because it did not feature at all. Linda recognized this so we arranged to do a Harvest assembly together. As we met to prepare this, at only our second meeting, I simply asked how she was, as Linda seemed to me to be very tired, with what I felt was a grey-tinged weariness. At this point she burst into floods of tears and I sat with her as she sobbed. Eventually Linda said that she had been doing this demanding job for two years and I was the first person ever to ask her how she was as a person. For the first time in two years she felt cared for; and this led Linda, slowly but surely, on a journey of faith in which she recovered a spiritual dimension to her life and found new ways to express it.

And it all began with an expression of genuine care. It does appear to be true that 'the human race can only survive because people care' (Virgo 1987: 11). The rabbis of the Mishnah suggest that 'when people are created in the image of God they are all different. What they hold in common is simply their infinite value, from which the rabbis derived the rule that one who saves a single life is as if he had saved the entire universe' (Sacks 1995: 108–9). That is one reason for writing this book. I hope also that it will be of value to anyone who cares in any capacity in a church or faith community, for two other reasons.

The first is that we need to recognize and honour the vital role caring people play in the faith community. In offering the care they contribute not only to the health of that community but to that of the worldwide community as well. They help provide a shelter, albeit temporary, from the hurricanes and storms that ravage and damage so many people's lives. They help provide the life-saving first aid that stems a bleeding artery until more experienced help arrives. As a young person new to motorbikes I ran a Suzuki 125cc for a year before checking and then changing the oil. Nobody had told me this was an essential feature for the mechanical health of a motorbike, although I did learn when I saw various metal flakes in the treacle-like oil that was eventually coaxed out of the gearbox. It all made sense: the lack of performance; the overheating engine and the increased noise and vibration. All of this could have been avoided if I had paid attention to some simple but vital care of my machine. People, even more than machines, require that same level of simple but vital pastoral care in 'the great unchangeables of human existence: birth, death, love, companionship and faith' (Goodliff 1998: 117).

Secondly, the pastoral care we give can always be improved and become more effective without a radical change in our identity as pastoral carers. There may be something seductive and attractive about the word 'counsellor' or 'psychotherapist', and indeed many people want to train as one or the other. To be a counsellor might imply wisdom, knowledge and an insight into the depths of human emotion, and that has a widespread appeal. But there are many more people who are able to exercise care, which is equally wise, knowing, and insightful. We could use the analogy of pastoral care being the fence at the top of a cliff that prevents people from falling, rather than being a specialist rescue centre for the fallen victims.

Defining pastoral care

The word 'pastoral' needs explanation in our supermarket, pre-packed culture, where what we eat is distanced from those who produce it. The term is figurative and metaphorical; describing God's care of his people in agricultural terms where God is the shepherd and we are the sheep. The term 'pastoral' then brings together the practical and the spiritual and was expressed historically as 'the cure of souls'. Caring for others – the meaning of 'cure of souls' – is the pastoral task of being 'accountable for shepherding the inner life of the people through the crises of emotional conflict and interpersonal pain towards growth in responsiveness towards God' (Oden 1983: 187) – God in this context is the ultimate being of religious faith.

The well-founded critique of such a definition is that it puts the emphasis on a religious professional such as a minister or rabbi (Campbell 1986: 23). A more inclusive definition sees pastoral care as *the activities of an individual or a group acting (as an expression of their religious beliefs) in a way that helps others, from outside as well as within their own faith community. This help may be practical, spiritual or both. The end product of pastoral care is that the person has passed through a situation of crisis or change with their whole being – body, mind and spirit – having been attended to.* Lyall (2001: 11ff.) helpfully explores the constellation of ideas, values, beliefs and traditions that construct the pastoral paradigm. By identifying these parameters Lyall shows how we can avoid a danger pointed out by Campbell (1987: 189ff.)

> The high aim of pastoral care for human well-being must be qualified by an awareness of its limits. The pastoral ministry . . . is carried out in a complex world [and] . . . a confidence in the omni-competence of pastoral care must be avoided. Often the most caring pastoral act is referral to other persons or agencies better qualified to act.

Giving someone a lift to see their GP, waiting for them and then letting them tell their story of the last hour is real pastoral care. Praying with someone facing redundancy or hospitalization are other real examples of pastoral care. But praying with someone diagnosed with manic depression and telling them to come off their medication as they are going to be healed is not responsible pastoral care and falls into the trap mentioned by Campbell. On the other hand, suggesting that they talk through their issues with a pastoral counsellor is responsible pastoral care.

In the last thirty years the word 'pastoral' has become widely used in education to refer to the welfare of students, with no particular religious reference. However, in this book the faith dimension of 'pastoral' is a vital, though not intrusive, component.

Defining church and faith communities

The word 'church' means literally the assembly of God's people – from the Bible concepts have developed of the church as the people of God, a living, communal expression of the body of Christ, marked by the presence of the Holy Spirit. The word church is often associated with a building or a particular expression or denomination of the Christian faith, eg the Church of England. As different representations of the church have specific beliefs – eg the Roman Catholic Church has certain views about the origin of life and abortion – I refer to these by their specific name.

The word 'faith' according to Cantwell Smith can mean 'an orientation of the personality, to oneself, to one's neighbour, to the universe, a total response' (quoted in Jacobs 1995a: 166). This total response need not be religious and is found in many human activities. Football fans can have 'faith' in their team, despite evidence to the contrary week by week. Clients can have 'faith' in their counsellor, believing that through this unique relationship they will find the help they are looking for. I use the word 'faith' primarily to describe the 'human response to the presence and activity of the transcendent' (Webster 1993: 208). What gives shape and meaning to this faith is the context in which it is held or experienced, so a faith community is a vital framework. A faith community is a specific, organized group of people in which a series of religious beliefs and values are adhered to as an expression of individual and corporate faith. So while a faith community may also be a church, I use the expression to describe all such faith groups, not restricting it to the Christian faith.

Carers with a context

Pastoral care and counsel has as its context the history, traditions, beliefs and values of a faith community. At the beating heart of every faith is a core of beliefs that define that particular religion, and as such give it a unique shape, colour and texture. The moment of drama when a priest declares with outstretched hands over bread and wine a prayer that transforms the material to the spiritual; the sheer historical wealth and present-day intimacy of a Jewish family beginning Pesach or Passover celebrations with the words 'Mah nishtanah halaylah hazeh mikol haleylot?' (Why is this night different from all the other nights?); the silent moments when the words of a preacher become the very word of God and all space and time appear to stand still; the cry of the Imam calling the faithful Moslem to prayer; these snapshots of some aspects of religious life contain within them an image shaped by profound beliefs, which, like blood in a human body, pulse with life throughout any religious organism and organization. To use another image, they are dynamic representations of belief more like a movie preview than a static photographic image. Often religious belief is presented in static terms, a slavish adherence to a legal code, which detracts from life and reduces belief to dogma. Belief is rather a process from the theoretical to the actual, from the 'out there' to 'in here', from the transcendent to the incarnate, from the written narrative account contained in the Bible, the Torah, the Talmud or Mishnah to the personal narrative of a person's life. Paradoxically, in order for anything to be a belief, it needs to be trusted and acted upon as well as believed. You can believe Henry VIII had six wives or that Elvis Presley was abducted by aliens without this information requiring any action: such beliefs do not impinge on our lives. When a potential belief (no matter how true it is) becomes an actual belief, it is an exciting moment, one that invokes awe and is often enshrined within religious traditions. Abstract truth becomes actual truth as it is recognized and acted upon. Much religious tradition concerns the maintenance and preservation of abstract truth, whereas my focus in this book is the point at which living truth happens, when theory becomes reality, when life events force us or expose us to discover what faith is really all about.

The role of faith community leaders

Within each faith community there is a central figure: the priest, pastor, clergy-person, rabbi, imam, guru and master. Some of these religious leaders are at the pinnacle of a faith structure and play a role in maintaining and supporting that structure. There may arise considerable tensions between the needs of an individual and those of the faith community. The fact that such a figure exists is important, especially in a culture and time when individualism dominates and everyone acts as a permanent consumer. The words 'faith community' are a reminder of our essential need to belong to a community, which transcends the crippling isolation of much contemporary existence. These observations raise three particular problems for such a leader, which I and others as ministers of one church or another have encountered. They are not insurmountable problems but they are real and may even indicate that those who do not have such a specific role within the faith community can often provide the most effective pastoral care and counselling. These problems concern, first, the representative role of the leader in relation to the wider community; second, time pressures and expectations; and third, the dynamics between people when one of them has a specifically religious role.

With respect to the first issue, there are times when a faith community leader or representative will hold a belief on behalf of that community which conflicts so profoundly with the individual's issues that it is difficult to reconcile the two.

Mary was deeply distressed. Between her sobs she cried 'I know what I believe. My beliefs are important to me and that's the problem. If they are true then what I'm doing is wrong. But you probably don't understand how I feel. For the first time in my life I feel alive, I've discovered feelings I didn't know existed before, so what can I do? I want to carry on with my faith but the two just don't fit together. What can I do? Do I, like an ostrich, stick my head in the sand and pretend that nothing has happened? Do I split myself in two and become a Jekyll and Hyde figure? Am I just going to become a hypocrite who says one thing and does another? Do I really have to make a choice?' Mary was

> expressing her confusion about having an affair with a man who loved
> her, rather than remaining faithful to her physically abusive alcoholic
> husband.

Or, to take other examples, should Paul 'come out' about his
ambivalent, and possibly homosexual, sexuality? Can Susie use
contraceptives to prevent pregnancy, when she already has three
children under the age of three? These are some simple moral or
ethical questions with which pastoral carers in a wide range of
faith communities become engaged. These questions do not
usually have simple answers, and are multiplied over and over
when we begin to think about specific areas of belief. Can a
daughter say Kaddish (a mourner's prayer) at her father's funeral?
Is the ordination of women to ministry biblical? Can Protestant
evangelical and Roman Catholic churches cooperate? It is so
much easier to ask the questions than to supply the answers. Yet a
leader of a faith community is often expected to provide the
answers; it is deemed to be part of her/his leadership of the community, of helping that community to be true to its faith position
and stated beliefs. The key issue is often less what they say than
how they say it. Jacobs illustrates this in his work on Fowler's
contribution to the psychology of religious belief.

> Since they are trained to fulfil a faith-leadership role one can
> assume they fall into one of two 'stages' of faith: there are
> those who see their tasks as guardians and interpreters, pro-
> viding answers to those who question, and are likely to
> defend their faith against anything that might undermine
> traditional beliefs and values ... There are other religious
> guides who have no particular axe to grind: they seek only to
> assist the individual find her or his own path. They do not
> impose standard beliefs and values, though they may
> point to some of the rich resources that can inform and
> enlighten ... What is more difficult is to find the religious
> leader or the faith community that is open to debate and
> doubt at a profound level.
>
> (1995a: 391–2)

Given this tension faced by faith leaders, pastoral care may well be better provided by others within the faith community who do not have the added burden of being a leader.

As an illustration of the second issue, imagine this scene, commonly experienced by ministers or rabbis. After conducting a service on a Sunday morning or on the Sabbath a queue forms of people wanting to see you. An elderly lady wants to tell you the story of her week, which, you know from previous experience, will be time-consuming. You want to talk to some new people to welcome them personally, whilst escaping the clutches of the first lady. As you edge across to intercept the new couple on their way out, another person darts in front, blocking your progress, and then proceeds to utter what sounds like a rehearsed speech about something that is troubling them about the church or synagogue. Before you can recover from this onslaught, a child tugs at your trouser leg wanting to show a new toy; you bend down to say 'hello', and as you stand up there looms the one person you didn't want to speak to who wants to continue the argument begun at a fraught meeting earlier in the week. The musicians want their music and songs for the evening service; the steward needs to give you a rota of readers; someone wants to be prayed for and so the demands stretch on and on. In this hectic process there are three casualties. The first is the faith leader. He or she is bombarded, because everyone wants something from her/him; as a consequence he or she may retreat emotionally and spiritually, giving as little as he or she hopes may satisfy each of the people who ask for some attention to their needs. It is not surprising that faith community leaders experience burnout or compassion fatigue, especially if they fail to recognize the full range of the demands placed on them. The second casualty is the faith leader's family, who bear a hidden cost (Coate 1989: 187–91). The third casualty is pastoral care. Mary Anne Coate in her book on clergy stress and the hidden conflicts of ministry has several chapters entitled 'the strain of . . .'. She talks about the strain of caring, proclaiming, relating to God and of 'being'. Pastoral care is only one aspect of a faith leader's role; and it may be the one that can most helpfully be delegated to others, who do not have the multifaceted cluster of demands from the whole faith community. Because they are free within that community to concentrate on the specific area of pastoral care, they are able to give greater focus and commitment to it.

A third serious issue for a faith leader who is also a counsellor is role confusion (Jacobs 1993a: 38). The client may be wondering, 'Is the person who is preaching or explaining the Torah speaking as a faith leader or my personal counsellor? Are they saying those words because they know more about me and are trying to tell me something they cannot say elsewhere? How can I take communion when the minister knows what I have thought and done in the last few weeks?' An even more complicated dynamic is the psychological process called transference. Transference happens when a person, usually unconsciously, transposes on to the faith leader emotions which they had experienced earlier in life in relation to a significant person such as a parent or a partner. Transference feelings often polarize into good 'positive' transference and bad 'negative' transference. For example, an adult who was abused as a child may transfer negative feelings about the abuser on to the faith leader. So if a faith leader experiences an exaggerated reaction that seems inappropriate, confusing or alarming, one important reason may be that a transference reaction is occurring.

Kevin moved to a new parish as its vicar and after a warm welcome got on with his responsibilities. Everything seemed to be going well apart from a problem with the church cleaner. He gave her time, listened to her complaints, supported her role at a parochial church council meeting and thought that they had developed a good working relationship. Soon, however, other problems surfaced and she became very critical of him. He could not work out what was happening. Later he met his predecessor at a conference and discovered that he had experienced similar problems with her. Kevin explored this process with a colleague who provided pastoral supervision and they came to a conclusion: it turned out that the cleaner had once been married to a wealthy, dynamic businessman, and had lived in a big house in the village. They had been through an acrimonious divorce after which she had moved to the less fashionable outskirts of the village. Kevin and his family lived in a substantial vicarage not far from the cleaner's former house. He came to the church with the reputation of being a dynamic leader. As he pieced this together using his supervisor's suggested concept of transference, Kevin saw that in many ways he was similar to the cleaner's former husband, and the acrimony and hurt experienced by her were coming out in her present relationship with him. Despite knowing this, there was little Kevin could do and eventually the cleaner was replaced, repeating at another level what had happened to her before.

The presence of transference leads some to conclude that a counselling role is not appropriate for a minister (Krebs quoted in Lyall 1995: 57), whilst others continue to see it as an important function.

> The minister is a living moving target for transference by many people when that minister is functioning as preacher, priest, teacher and even in short-term pastoral counselling . . . Since we ministers, as a result of our own particular and unique relationships with persons, do receive emotions and fantasies and expectations which were originally learned earlier in relationship to others, a part of our competence is the ability to recognize this when it takes place and to respond to others with genuineness in the reality of the present.
>
> (Switzer quoted in Lyall 1995: 58)

In my own experience it is much more difficult to recognize what is taking place in relationship to transference than Switzer suggests; and for the sake of clarity of boundaries I would no longer see people for counselling in a church where I belong either as a leader or a member. These different difficulties can leave the faith leader feeling less than integrated, and in contradiction to the faith so clearly professed. Is there another way of managing these issues? The concept of 'holding' is important in the therapeutic world (see Winnicott 1990 and Jacobs 1995b) and it can have vital pastoral application.

'Holding relationship' as pastoral care

One of the vital tasks performed by a mother for a child described by Winnicott is that of 'holding'. Gomez amplifies this:

> Holding is both physical and emotional. The good-enough mother contains and manages the baby's feelings and

impulses by empathising with him and protecting him from too many jarring experiences ... the mother's holding enables the baby's 'true self', the spontaneous experience of being, to develop coherence and continuity.

(Gomez 1997: 89)

At times, then, there will be tension, disagreement or conflict between individual needs, beliefs and values, and group or community needs, beliefs and values. In effect the pastoral caring role can provide a 'holding environment or relationship', which gives security for a person in their vulnerability, crisis or doubt. It encourages the emotional and spiritual dimensions of a person's true self to emerge. Some pastoral care begins with the person, discovering their hopes, hurts, fears and joys and then moves, often slowly, towards enabling that person to become integrated with their faith context and within their faith community. Or it can begin with a particular faith tradition or understanding and work towards applying this in the complex and often chaotic life experience of each person. Both directions are possible and both are demanding, often accompanied by the perpetual feeling of being stretched between two seemingly opposing forces and the nagging fear of becoming detached from both. This book is intended to help pastoral carers to span this gap, to create sufficient space for fresh perspectives, and to develop a 'holding environment or relationship'.

My aim is to provide additional resources for those who practise pastoral care – resources drawn from the counselling and therapeutic world – to equip them further and help them in their ongoing task of care. It is not my intention to turn carers into amateur counsellors, something that requires different and equally specialized training. My first attempt at repairing my first motorbike (other than changing the oil) highlights one of the issues about learning to practise pastoral care properly. It was very easy to dismantle the engine, taking less than an hour, but enormously difficult to reassemble it in the days that followed. And I was trying to do this with a hammer and a screwdriver and the three spanners that came in the toolkit with the motorbike. What I really needed was an instruction manual, a proper set of spanners and a socket set. This book aims to offer a set of skills to help in the vital pastoral task of care and counsel in church and faith communities, so that pastoral carers can become even more effective. I also aim to enable the reader to know when it is time to refer someone to a person with more specialized expertise and training. One of the skills of pastoral care is to enable people to seek the right kind of help at the right time.

What follows is in two parts. The first and major section focuses on counselling skills, drawing on insights and illustrations from pastoral contexts. The counselling skills are presented in the form of an integrative skills model, drawn from different theoretical traditions, which sees the pastoral encounter as having three (initial, intermediate, closing) phases. Chapters 2 to 5 provide an overview of person-centred, psychodynamic and narrative therapies and introduce the tasks, skills and relational qualities required in the initial stage of using counselling skills as a pastoral carer. Chapters 6 to 8 explore the intermediate stage of pastoral skills, showing how a use of basic skills and personal qualities can be combined to bring about a greater pastoral contribution to the life of others. Chapters 9 to 11 examine the ending stage, with a practical focus being on loss (a subject frequently encountered in pastoral care and counselling).

The second section, Chapters 12 to 14, covers key issues that occur in a pastoral context: conflicts with beliefs and values; power and sexuality; and guilt, shame and forgiveness. It is of course impossible to cover every eventuality, because each person to whom care is offered is unique. But there are some useful principles, which come from slightly different counselling approaches, and it is to these that the focus initially turns.

Part One

Counselling skills in the pastoral context

Chapter **2**

Counselling skills for pastoral carers

Many people in church and faith communities offer their pastoral care through the use of counselling skills, but they are not counsellors. Counselling is regulated by professional bodies, principally the British Association for Counselling and Psychotherapy (BACP). That organization, of which the Association for Pastoral and Spiritual Care and Counselling is a division, also has a code of practice which includes the use of counselling skills. Since counselling skills are an important aspect of pastoral and spiritual care, the next three chapters concentrate on what these are and how they may be practised. I introduce a three-stage integrative skills model based on relationship. This chapter focuses on counselling models that can be integrated in the pursuit of counselling skills.

According to the definition used by BACP, counselling skills are being used when there is an 'intentional use of specific interpersonal skills' similar to those found in counselling; when the role of the person using those skills is 'enhanced without being changed'; and the person being helped perceives the helper in his/her caring role and not as a counsellor. For example, at a wedding reception, following a service which I had conducted, I was seated at the top table next to one of the bridesmaids. As time went on I learnt more about Wendy and her eventful life. I listened, reflected back to her what she was saying in a summarized way that also drew on the emotion she was expressing. Wendy said at one point 'How do you know so much about me?' and I replied that it was because she had told me so much about herself. All I had done was to listen to her words and her emotions. This was a brief pastoral encounter brought about by my role as a minister. I did not have any responsibilities for this person beyond being there when she needed someone to listen to her sadness about why her relationships never worked out. This was not counselling, but I was using some counselling skills.

One of the dangers of picking up skills is not seeing how they all fit together. Imagine trying to do a jigsaw puzzle without a picture to help work out where each piece goes. I set out below a framework of counselling skills that I have developed as a conceptual grid to provide a more professional application of them. This is an integrated skills model combining three different approaches used in counselling itself: person-centred, psychodynamic, and narrative counselling, with a focus on the actual skills they employ. In many brief pastoral encounters the focus on the initial stage is all that is required. When there is ongoing contact with a person, it may be appropriate to make use of the skills found in the intermediate or closing stages of this integrative model. If someone requires more help than this model can provide they are likely to require help from another person outside their immediate pastoral situation. Since this model combines terms and skills from three major counselling approaches, it is also useful to see what these represent and how they may be relevant to pastoral and spiritual care.

Person-centred counselling

Carl Rogers founded this form of counselling, which is also known as client-centred counselling. The key aspects are that the counsellor is non-directive and reflective. He or she does not give advice or interpretations except to clarify or encourage something the client is saying. The assumption behind this is that the client is the person who is the expert on his/her life and knows what is best. People often need time to discover this confidence for themselves and this is best done in an atmosphere of acceptance and a relationship that is non-judgemental. The basic concepts of person-centred counselling include: the incongruence of the client (that is, that they do not feel themselves); the congruence of the counsellor (that is, someone who is deeply in touch with themselves); and three core conditions of unconditional positive regard, empathy and genuineness. Working with these concepts may enable the client to function more fully and experience self-actualization. There is a specific focus on the 'here and now' relationship between the client and the counsellor, or what the existential philosopher and theologian Martin Buber called 'the I/Thou relationship' (Smith 1966).

From a faith perspective this is a challenging approach for someone with pastoral responsibility. Some religious people feel a need to defend and promote their particular faith or belief and find it difficult to work in a way that concentrates only on what the 'client' says and believes. They want to put across their own truth, and direct the other person towards it (see Chapter 12). At this stage it is important to observe that if people do not feel they have been heard or listened to, at a depth which acknowledges them as real persons rather than as people with a faith problem for which the carer thinks there is a solution, they are less likely to feel valued as part of the faith community.

Psychodynamic counselling

Psychodynamic counselling draws its theoretical basis from the psychoanalytic tradition inaugurated by Freud and refined by post-Freudian thinkers, such as Klein and Winnicott. The term 'psychodynamic' points to something dynamic and vital that happens within a person's psyche. 'Psyche' can be translated a number of ways, but I take psyche to represent that interplay of body, mind and spirit that has made and still makes us who we are. The word also suggests that something dynamic happens in our encounters with others; and these can, in the right circumstances, provide further insight into who we are. Psychodynamic counselling holds together a theoretical understanding of a dynamic process with a practical concern to make or provide the environment in which people may explore their past, present and future, principally through their relationship with another. The basic concepts of psychodynamic counselling include: conflict and unconscious processes; anxiety and psychic pain; defence mechanisms; motivational drives; developmental phases; models of the mind; and therapeutic relationships. There is a specific focus on the 'back there and then' relationship expressed through 'transference' that takes place here and now between the client and the counsellor.

From a faith perspective this is an equally challenging perspective for someone with pastoral responsibility. The realization that someone seeking pastoral help might relate to the carer as someone significant from their past can lead to powerful feelings, both positive and negative. A person may idealize a religious figure, such as a priest, minister, rabbi or imam, so that he or she becomes all-powerful, all-knowing, and is even imbued with divine authority. This is a powerful dynamic and may facilitate great healing in a person's life, but it also introduces the possibility of great harm. Transference happens to some extent with all authority figures, such as doctors or teachers, but there is particular danger when it is combined with the powerful role of the leader in a faith community. As I have already suggested, in some ways the best pastoral care can be done by people who do not have a specific authority role, since this lessens the possibility of such powerful transference, which, while it may be a useful tool in counselling and psychotherapy, is less so in pastoral care and the use of counselling skills.

Narrative counselling

This form of counselling has become an important element in various approaches. It reflects in part the way we live in society in today's postmodern times. 'In everyday life we are surrounded by stories. We tell ourselves and each other stories all of the time. We structure, store and communicate our experiences through stories. We live in a culture that is saturated with stories: myths, novels, TV soaps, office gossip, family histories and so on' (McLeod 1997, 1998: 144). The term 'story' conveys a structured account, with a beginning, a middle and an end, which communicates drama, emotion and something about the teller and the characters within. McLeod argues that the term 'narrative' is a general term linking several stories, interpretations, explanations and commentaries. 'The whole of what a client says in a counselling session can therefore be seen as his or her "narrative", which may be built around the telling of three or four discrete "stories" over the course of the hour' (1997, 1998: 146).

Within all religious traditions, the telling of stories recorded in special texts, with subsequent drawing on these through interpretations, explanations and commentaries, has been a vital expression of faith. It has led, in the Christian tradition, to the development of narrative theology. When the world of the text impinges upon the world of the reader, interpretation transforms the reader's world by offering a new way of understanding. Translated into pastoral language this means the pastoral counsellor or carer is engaged in a counselling session at more than a psychological level. As the counsellor encounters the client's story, expressed in metaphors, narratives, poetic language and what Vanhoozer (1998) calls 'Gospel truths', the process engenders a new way of being that finds its best expression in hope. For Christians, the narrative of this suffering and hope contained in God and God's people finds its ultimate expression in their identification with the life, death and resurrection of Jesus Christ. Hope is found because God has experienced suffering, though Fiddes cautions us, 'If God's suffering is to be of healing effect for a suffering world, then it must be recognisably God's, and not merely human suffering projected on to God' (1988: 110). The focus in terms of counselling skills linked to narrative therapy is on the need to listen to other people, hear them, and enable them to speak of the beginning, middle and end of their own story in the context of their faith story.

An integrative skills model

Drawing on different aspects of these person-centred, psychodynamic and narrative traditions, it is possible to construct an integrative skills model. The following diagram sets out the key focus or task of a pastoral encounter, the skills that are required and the relational qualities that underpin these. These three aspects are related to three stages in pastoral care: the initial, the intermediate and the closing stages.

The danger of any model is that it can become too neat, with people fitted into each stage and section. What is unusual about working in a faith community is that while pastoral encounters

Table 1.1 An integrated model for pastoral skills

Helping skills: a relational approach	Starting out – the initial stage	Moving on – the intermediate stage	Letting go – the closing stage
Tasks	1 Establishing a helping relationship or working alliance 2 Clarifying the problems or issues 3 Making some form of assessment 4 Understanding the client's internal frame of reference 5 Clarifying guidelines or boundaries 6 Enabling a narrative to be told	1 Maintaining and developing the helping relationship 2 Overcoming resistance to change 3 Working on the problems or issues 4 Facilitating new perspectives 5 Linking past and present 6 Maintaining boundaries 7 Discovering new aspects of personal and emotional narrative	1 Bringing to a close a piece of work 2 Being aware of repeat losses and their impact 3 Enabling the person to be more authentic or integrated 4 Changing boundaries 5 Resourcing new aspects of personal and emotional narrative

Skills	1 Listening to six key areas 2 Active listening using reflecting back and paraphrasing 3 Making connections: 'it seems as if . . .' 4 Containing or bracketing our external frame of reference	1 Communicating 'core values' 2 Employing perceptive immediacy 3 Using metaphors or simple interpretations 4 Using challenge or confrontation in a way that enables progress	1 Being clear about endings and keeping these in focus 2 Understanding the emotional impact of loss 3 Establishing what the person has gained and now values in him or herself
Relational qualities	1 Being real and concrete 2 Being present and immediate 3 Expressing acceptance and empathy 4 Self-awareness	1 Staying with the person, especially when they get 'stuck' 2 Avoiding taking responsibility for the client 3 Expressing non-possessive warmth	1 Letting go and bearing ambivalence and anger 2 Believing in self, others and being 'good enough'

using these skills are occasional and informal, the person is often also part of a community, so that it is possible to work issues with him or her over a matter of weeks, months or even years as the following example shows.

Ian (a Methodist pastoral visitor) went to see Irene, a 44-year-old woman, in hospital where she was to have a hysterectomy. She was feeling nervous and wanted him to pray with her before the operation, which she dreaded. Irene told Ian that the last time she had been in hospital was for the delivery of her son, now a teenager. She reflected on all the changes that had taken place in her life over the previous fifteen years, including a painful and protracted divorce. Ian listened and helped Irene see how her faith helped but did not obliterate her past. She said she valued the prayer and the visit and Ian went on his way. Irene resumed her attendance at church and found her friends to be understanding and helpful. She even felt able to become part of the pastoral visiting team as she felt she could use her experience to help others. Several months later, Irene found herself getting very upset for no apparent reason. This time Ian visited her at her home and, as he listened to her, reflected back that any operation has physical, emotional and spiritual impact. She knew 'in her head' that this operation was necessary, but found herself feeling she had been robbed of the possibility of a future child. This led Irene into talking about her need for a new partner and the loneliness and responsibility she was feeling as a single parent. A year later Irene rang Ian and could hardly contain her excitement as she told him that she had met a new man and they had been out for a 'date'. Later that year their marriage took place and after some thought they decided to move away, but before Irene left she told Ian how important the pastoral relationship had been for her. She could see a definite beginning of trust but had allowed that to deepen and help her see important connections in her life, both psychologically and spiritually.

Irene's growth as a person had been helped by the pastoral skills used by Ian over a period of time and the caring context of the faith community. As Irene moved away into a new phase of her life she felt sad at the ending of her relationship with Ian but empowered by the new insights she had gained about herself which deepened what she could offer to others. The chapters that follow develop these skills and qualities, so that they can be practised in a way that leads both to personal growth and a new resourcing for the pastoral care tradition held by various faith communities.

Chapter 3

Starting out – the initial stage of pastoral skills

Tasks

This description of the opening stage of using counselling skills can be split for clarity into three sections, although they are obviously interwoven in practice. The skills and relational qualities required for this initial stage are covered in Chapters 4 and 5 respectively. Here I examine certain tasks that need to be undertaken if there is to be a productive use of counselling skills.

1 Establishing a helping relationship or working alliance

This seems like common sense although, as Anna Freud once commented, 'the trouble with common sense is that it is so rare'. We assume that a pastoral carer is there to help the other person. Unfortunately this is not always so. Sometimes people who work as carers have adopted this role because they are more in need of care themselves (see Chapter 11).

Julia was always the first person to volunteer for any task that was announced in the church. When a new scheme of pastoral visitors was put in place, she was first in the queue. The new minister at first thought this was helpful. However, over the year, when he had further pastoral contact with individuals who had been visited by Julia, he heard the same story. Julia went to see people to support them but always ended up talking more about herself than listening to their concerns. In some cases they ended up helping Julia out emotionally and financially. When the time came, a year later, to review the pastoral scheme, the minister found himself in 'hot water' because he refused to allow Julia to continue as a pastoral visitor. He tried challenging Julia about the way she appeared to use her pastoral care to meet her needs and not those of the people she was visiting. Julia became very defensive and tearful and stormed out of the meeting. The next week he received a number of calls from the people Julia had visited complaining at his 'high-handed' attitude. It soon transpired that Julia had visited all of them and encouraged them to call on her behalf, giving them a one-sided account.

Every community has someone like Julia – someone who meets his or her own needs under the guise of helping of others. Unfortunately this does not help because at heart the helper is not there for the other person. It is essential before using counselling skills that we are clear that a helping relationship is established primarily for the good of the other rather than the helper. Only when this is established is it possible to begin to develop a working alliance. Whilst this has a specific meaning in psychodynamic counselling (Jacobs 1988: 99–100) it is also a concise way of expressing the focus for counselling skills. It highlights the need for partnership, which is a fundamental aspect of all good pastoral care and counselling. Experience suggests that if this aspect is missing, anything that is accomplished is accidental rather than intentional. Research has shown that the personal qualities that facilitate the development of a working alliance include: genuineness and warmth; naturalness and a sense of humour; a recognition that the helper does not have all the answers; a willingness to recognize the painful material that people share; straightforward, ordinary language and an openness to learn (Robbins in Patton and Meara 1992).

2 Clarifying the problems or issues

The theologian David Ford talks about the pressures and demands in society as 'multiple overwhelmings'. When people ask for help or are simply overcome with emotion, they do not always know why. They have reached a point of being overwhelmed, and the initial pastoral task requiring counselling skills is to understand what the problem is.

Mandy was at her best friend's wedding when she bumped into Gavin, another old friend from university. Gavin in his career as a teacher had learnt to listen to people and was pastoral head of a year group. The story she told him was about mixed feelings – of celebrating for her best friend and the joy of the day, alongside the pain and confusion of her longing for a partner. 'Who needs *Bridget Jones's Diary* when you can have my life?' she exclaimed. 'Oh God, I don't believe I actually said that' were her next embarrassed words. Gavin asked gently what it was she wanted? 'Someone to listen who won't think I am going mad' was her answer. Mandy did not want Gavin to solve her problem or arrange a blind date. Her need was more immediate – to have someone reassure her that her internal turmoil did not mean she was going mad. 'You must think I'm a right cow?' she went on to say, presumably because she was envious of her friend as well. Gavin said briefly that it was understandable to experience powerful conflicting feelings such as she had described in the previous twenty minutes. Several hours later, as the evening ended, Mandy went up to Gavin, thanked him, and kissed him on the cheek. 'I've learnt a lot today. Thanks for being there', she said. Mandy had been able to focus on her need and allow this to surface, and to separate it from her feelings for her best friend.

---

3 Making some form of assessment

'Assessment' is a word rarely used in the context of pastoral care. While it plays a very important role in counselling (McLeod 1998: 222), its absence from pastoral care may be one of the factors hindering the effectiveness of some of the work done. This need for assessment challenges the assumption that any person (with God or the Torah on their side) can handle any situation and any person. 'If only they had more faith' is one response heard in some church contexts. 'Why go to secular counsellors when God has given us the Holy Spirit?' is another all too common response.

Both these responses assume the all-sufficiency of a faith tradition. Pastoral care, if it is to retain its integrity, must pursue a degree of professionalism, which helpers from other disciplines can respect. The willingness to recognize that not everyone can be helped, or that the person needs a more specialized form of help, is a key factor.

Jerry wandered in to the coffee morning held in the church hall. He looked dishevelled and smelt of urine, much to the consternation of the regular clientele. John was the carer on duty and he went and sat down with this stranger, discovered his name and fetched him a cup of coffee and some cake. During the morning John listened to Jerry and, despite feeling that he was doing little good, was able to piece together something of Jerry's history. He had recently been discharged from psychiatric care and was finding it difficult to fit into the community. John did not feel a need to offer any spiritual resource such as prayer, or any well-intentioned advice. He recognized that Jerry needed more support, which was available elsewhere, so, after a telephone call, he walked with him to a MIND mental health centre half a mile down the road. John was aware that he did not have the experience to do more than listen, yet he was able to make an initial assessment that Jerry needed significant help for his mental health issues. John did in fact offer real 'care in the community'. Several months later a barely recognizable Jerry returned to the coffee morning asking for John. John scrutinized the clean, alert person before him as Jerry told him how much better he had been since going back on his medication. He explained that, when they first met, he had been thinking about ending his life, so great was his despair. John's act of kindness had been a turning point for him. Jerry still has his mental health problems to contend with and many challenges to face, yet on that occasion he had found help when he needed it.

It is vital to acknowledge that we cannot help everyone: we need the ability to ask whether some people would be better helped by someone with more specialist knowledge and experience.

4 Understanding the client's internal frame of reference

This sounds technical but is straightforward enough. A frame of reference is the way we see and make sense of our world, and it is different for every single person.

I work with twins and their parents and provide counselling support for the Birmingham Twins Clinic. As this brings me into regular contact with twins, triplets and their parents I have learnt to see events from a particular perspective. One 3-year-old twin, Claire, asked her mother what had happened to the other one when her neighbour gave birth to just one baby. Until then Claire had always thought that babies came in pairs, an understandable enough view reflecting her experience. Being a twin gave her a particular frame of reference by which she thought she understood other mothers and babies.

A pastoral carer who uses counselling skills has often had previous contact with the person he or she is helping. This informs us about them: in a pastoral context we often know other family members, friendships, beliefs, attitudes, experiences they have gone through, all of which help form an unspoken background to the present situation. Because of this informal knowledge, we have an advantage over the counsellor who has to maintain professional boundaries. But we should never take such knowledge for granted. We need to know what each person thinks now, not what someone else has said about them in the past, or what they may have told us in a different context, such as a study group where others are listening. This also applies to ethnic and racial issues, about which pastoral carers often have much to learn.

Mike recalled his first funeral for a Jamaican woman. Having conducted funerals before, he thought he was prepared; but he found himself overwhelmed by the immediacy of the grief, the turbulent emotion, the absolute sense of loss that were present on this occasion. At the time he felt, somewhat defensively, that it was all 'over the top'. But gradually he learnt that such grief is immensely healthy and may even be preferable to the stilted, reverential, repressed feelings in many white families.

This frame of reference includes an understanding of the client's church or faith community context, which is a vital part of the pastoral encounter.

> On a counselling skills course one of the students, Esther, was a rebutzin, the wife of rabbi. In one of the experiential exercises, in which they all had to sit in a circle and hold hands, Esther moved seats so that she did not have to hold hands with a man, since this was not acceptable within her Jewish faith.

People from a Christian faith background can also have difficulties in understanding others. It is common for Christians from the evangelical wing of the church to seek out a *Christian* counsellor (if they seek out a counsellor at all), rather than a secular counsellor, regardless of the individual's qualifications. Some say that they simply want someone who will understand their worldview, who does not see Christian faith as in any way pathological. This is not unreasonable, since in secular, psychiatric and academic settings being a Christian is often regarded as something strange. It is currently acceptable to be 'spiritual' – a term that is increasingly used in counselling circles – but still unacceptable to be 'religious'. In fact, the assumption is questionable that a Christian counsellor has an 'added dimension' that will somehow make the counselling different. Sometimes having a faith position makes it difficult to see through the defences and collusions for which we may be using our faith.

5 Clarifying guidelines or boundaries

Pastoral care is usually done in an unstructured way and demands great flexibility. It includes a casual conversation with someone at the local shopping centre; a hospital visit; seeing someone in their own home; writing a letter to someone who has not been around for a time; a telephone call expressing interest or concern, etc. What each of these situations contains is the possibility that 'previously hidden needs of the other person may become clear' (Boyd and Lynch 1999: 64). This very flexibility is intrinsic to pastoral care yet it also places great demands and significant tensions when counselling skills are introduced. Nowhere is this more obvious than in the area of boundaries. It has been argued that it is the nature of these boundaries that defines the difference between pastoral care and pastoral counselling (Boyd and Lynch 1999: 70–1).

Pastoral counselling is a helping relationship based on an explicitly agreed, firm set of boundaries. Pastoral care, on the other hand, is a form of helping relationship in which the boundaries of the relationship are typically left unspoken. In summarized form here is how Boyd and Lynch (1999) compare pastoral care and counselling:

Pastoral counselling	*Pastoral care*
Involves an explicit contract or agreement between the counsellor and the client on the terms on which they will work together	Does not normally involve any explicit contract between the pastoral carer and the person s/he is helping
The time, duration and frequency of the counselling sessions are agreed by the counsellor and client at the outset of the helping relationship	The time, duration and frequency of the meetings are typically flexible
A clear agreement is made between the counsellor and the client concerning the degree of confidentiality that the counsellor will be able to offer	There is not normally any explicit understanding concerning the confidentiality of the meetings
May involve the charging of a fee	Does not usually involve a fee
Counsellors require regular supervision from a person who is a trained and experienced counsellor	Pastoral carers may or may not receive regular supervision of their work; this supervision would not necessarily be with someone who is a trained counsellor

Boundaries are an extremely important subject: see Chapters 6 and 9. Here it is important to stress that pastoral carers need to be aware that there is something alluring about the role of counsellor. Sometimes people want to make those engaged in pastoral care into something they are not, and since sometimes we may want to make ourselves into something we are not, we can find ourselves in a difficult position that threatens to overstep the pastoral role. It is helpful to make explicit what we can and cannot undertake.

Jim, a pastoral carer, stood at the door of the church unsure what to do. He had noticed a man come into the back of the church. At the end of the service he went up to him, learnt that his name was Terry and tried to talk to him. Terry turned to Jim and demanded that he be exorcized, a request that Jim had never encountered before. Jim knew he could not do this but felt able to use his befriending skills. He said that he wasn't able to do an exorcism, suggested that Terry might be feeling very troubled, and asked whether he wanted to talk some more. Terry said he did and told Jim about his guilt (see Chapter 14) at causing the death of his wife. They had argued before she drove off and she was subsequently killed in a road accident. Terry felt he must be an evil person to cause his wife's death and he wanted to get rid of 'it', the 'it' being his guilt. Jim's clear boundary helped Terry find the appropriate focus for the help he so badly needed. If Jim had simply launched into a prayer, as a way of coping with a difficult situation that he did not know how to handle, it is very unlikely that Terry would have received the right kind of help. He might even have had his feeling of being 'evil' reinforced.

---

6 Enabling a narrative to be told

We live in a culture that at a philosophical level has rejected the 'big picture' and the concepts that once appeared to explain everything, at least in popular science and religion. We have developed instead a vicarious living of the life of others expressed through tabloid exposés, Hollywood idols, and the use of people's actual lives as television entertainment. The level of intrusiveness has reached new depths and is beyond anything that could at one time have been imagined outside Orwell's nightmare scenario of 'Big Brother' in his book *1984*.

Yet people want their own story to be told and remembered. In the film noir thriller of the 1950s, *Kiss Me Deadly*, the bleak paranoia of nuclear threat haunts and kills most of the characters in the film. A private eye picks up a disturbed, sobbing girl running down a dark highway escaping from some fearful past. She sends him a letter before her death with two words written on a single sheet of paper – 'Remember me.' People want to be remembered, and one way to achieve this is to share their story with another. Often this feels risky, for people fear their stories will be rejected.

George was an old soldier who had served in the Second World War. He had rarely spoken of his experiences, as he was part of a generation who 'got on with life' and regarded the past as past. During the VE celebrations a few years ago he found that he wasn't sleeping well. Dark dreams and memories, long forgotten, were surfacing. A reunion was organized for his regiment and he found himself increasingly anxious about attending. His grandson, who happened to be training as a psychiatrist, took him out for the day. In the space and privacy of a country pub away from the rest of the family George felt able to tell his grandson, of whom he was enormously proud, what he was feeling. George did not need medication and he had no psychiatric problems; it was enough that he felt safe with someone who listened to his story, including all the painful parts he had told no one else. This helped him enormously. He slept well; and he attended and enjoyed the reunion.

Every faith community probably has someone like George in its membership. George needed to talk about his past and bring it into the present, so that it became a coherent narrative, not just an interesting story of events that happened a long time ago and apparently bore no relation to life here and now. The pastoral role of enabling people to remember is enormously important and requires people who know how to listen. In some recent research into postnatal depression for women who had experienced a traumatic delivery, one conclusion was that good clinical care included giving women the opportunity to talk about their experience. 'All women deserve compassionate, kind, and competent clinical care during and after childbirth: when women seek opportunities to talk about their experiences of birth it is critical that someone has the time and the skills for listening' (Small and Lumley 2001: 928).

So there are six key tasks at this initial stage of our helping skills model. Each has a particular focus and application that is influenced by the pastoral context. The tasks that need to be achieved involve establishing a helping relationship, which results in being able to help the person in need to clarify his or her problem or issues. It involves making some form of assessment as to whether or not this person can be helped through pastoral care, which also requires the ability to understand his/her internal frame of reference or how he/she views the world. Given appropriate boundaries we can help the person tell his or her story in a way that brings meaning and value. The skills that are needed to accomplish these tasks are explained further in the next chapter.

Chapter 4

Starting out – the initial stage of pastoral skills

Skills

The skill of bread making appears to be resurgent amongst my friends and colleagues. When a clinical psychologist talks enthusiastically about kneading and a psychoanalytic psychotherapist extols the virtues of certain types of wheat grain, I wonder what it is I am missing. Others are opting for a more high-tech route, with breadmakers now becoming a common kitchen accessory. What I do know is that I enjoy the benefit of home-made bread whoever makes it. But people are not like a lump of dough that can be kneaded by a machine or even by the breadmaker. Pastoral skills enable people to find their own 'shape', and, in one sense – to pursue the biblical image – provide the right environment in which the leaven can work.

The pastoral encounter begins with the establishment of a helping relationship, which is different from a social relationship or a friendship, with their respective obligations. Out of this is formed a working alliance where both people, the helper and helped, work together and where the helper uses counselling skills to achieve this end. As the relationship develops, issues (including the client's church or faith community context) are clarified and understood from the client's perspective. Boundaries are established, and some form of assessment takes place in order to decide what is best for the person. The most effective way of accomplishing these tasks is to listen: listening is the focus of this second section of the initial phase. But note that while the temptation is to treat these counselling skills as a checklist, they cannot be learned as if they were some infallible guarantee of success.

1 Listening to six key areas

Listening takes place at a number of different but equally import-ant levels. The key areas are: content; feelings; the body; gender and sexuality; spirituality; and the social and political.

Content

It is common for students on counselling skills courses, where there is an emphasis on listening skills, to comment that they learn so much more when they concentrate on actually listening to another person. This listening involves three aspects: listening to what is being said, and not what we think or assume is being said; observing the person's non-verbal cues, the way they are standing or sitting, the tone of voice, their facial expres-sion and so on; and listening to the context of their current circumstances.

Feelings

People are often afraid of their emotions, yet it may be harmful to repress them. The purpose of listening to people's feelings is to get a clue as to what is really going on inside them especially if it is different from what they are saying. Non-verbal communication is one way of spotting this. The way people look and their tone of voice are often reliable indicators of their true state. When I was listening to Linda, the head teacher whose story opened this book, it was not what she said that made me ask how she felt, but what she had communicated by her tone of voice and her demeanour; she seemed to be carrying the weight of the world on her shoulders. Linda was genuinely feeling crushed by the enormity of her work and personal circumstances. Such non-verbal communication is all around us if we look for it, and monitor the response it evokes in us. When someone expresses a feeling it can resonate in us and inform us as to what may be going on, enabling us to listen to what lies just below the surface.

> Esther worked as a teacher within the Jewish community. Often her students told her about events in their lives. She was concerned about one person because he said so little, while she herself experienced powerful feelings of anger. The silence that emerged was being used in what felt like an angry way. She took the risk of coaxing it out of Ben. 'You don't seem to be very happy today. I think that there's a great deal happening in your life.' Ben burst into tears and it all poured out. He was angry and scared. He had overheard his parents talking about separation and he thought it must all be his fault. He was unhappy and angry that he couldn't make things better. By listening to her feelings Esther was able to provide Ben with a safe place to express his.

What Esther did was to listen to her own feelings and from this identify that she was not herself feeling angry about anything in particular. She understood that the psychological mechanism called 'projection' was taking place, which Jacobs describes as a kind of 'spitting out' (1993a: 166). Esther experienced Ben's angry feelings expressed in withdrawal and non-verbal communication that reflected how he was angry with his parents but could not express it. Ben was 'spitting out' his feelings psychologically in a way that Esther could make sense of. John Rowan, a humanistic counsellor comments: 'Of all the levels of listening, it is the emotional level which is the most important. It links, in a unique way, the earliest and the latest experience, the deepest and the shallowest, the most refined and the most earthy' (1983: 34).

People with a religious background may need particular help in discovering and expressing their emotions. This seems strange, since paradoxically a great deal of worship is emotional in content: there is dramatic tension as the priest proclaims that the bread and wine he or she holds have become the body and blood of Christ; the emotions are stirred as a choir or congregation sings; equally Judaism, in its festivals, celebrations and days of remembrance, has moments of profound emotion. Yet often when people of faith try to express their individual feelings (particularly those they deem to be negative and sinful) they find it difficult to do so. This emotional paralysis may result from issues of belief, authority, trust and fear, something I explore as part of a later stage. People often need some form of encouragement or permission to allow their emotions to surface, to be heard and valued.

The body

Sue was a very tall adolescent, who felt awkward about being a gangling six foot, taller than most of the boys in the youth group. This awkwardness was obvious in her body – she would stoop, with a hunched back, in order to avoid attention. The youth leaders were alert to this problem and made sure that Sue was given consideration without drawing attention to her height or making her the centre of attention. They helped her confidence by asking her to do tasks such as looking after the 'tuck shop', which made her feel genuinely useful. Slowly over a year Sue began to change and she joined in more of the activities and moved through to a more confident phase of later adolescence. She began to 'walk tall', as she would come into a room enjoying her height, feeling that it was part of her being and not something that embarrassed her. Sue's body demonstrated her inner struggle to be a confident person.

Any course or training on counselling skills covers the subject of body language. A person's body communicates a great deal, to which we may listen if we choose. Posture, facial expressions, tone of voice, laughter, smiles or tears, or other physiological response such as blushing all speak of what is going on inside. One aspect of the training of people who sell cars is a focus on body language. Salespersons have a very limited time in which to make a connection with a customer. They are taught, for example, to notice the specific gestures or responses that each of us displays, such as twisting a ring or fiddling with an earring; since buying a car is an anxiety-generating process, these gestures become more frequent or exaggerated. Research has revealed that if a person wants to know if another person likes them, they rely 7 per cent on the spoken word, 38 per cent on the tone of voice and 55 per cent on facial clues (Egan 1994: 95). Listening to the body – our own and that of the person we are helping – is therefore a crucial skill.

Gender and sexuality

> In the film *To Have and Have Not*, when Lauren Bacall first meets Humphrey Bogart, all she does is to say 'Anybody got a match?' Bogart coolly throws a box of matches across the room to her in the doorway. She lights a cigarette and casually throws the spent match over her shoulder, saying 'Thanks' huskily as she nonchalantly tosses the box back to him. It is not just the cigarette that is smouldering. This briefest of verbal exchanges communicates simmering passion and powerful emotion: in fact Bogart and Bacall actually fell in love during the making of the film.

Sexuality is a part of being human that should neither be denied nor exploited. In any helping encounter sexuality and gender are likely to play a part. Some religious traditions place prohibitions on men seeing women alone and this needs to be respected. Is sexuality so powerful that it overcomes all rational thought and religious observance (see Chapter 13)? Any person using counselling skills needs to have worked on their own understanding of their sexuality because it is present in all relationships, consciously or unconsciously. This does not mean that an intimate sexual encounter will result even though intimate feelings may be present. In the same way gender issues are always present. For example, many women have been badly used or abused by men; it is important therefore that they find a safe place where they can be heard. If they do not wish to talk about issues with a man, that wish should be respected.

Spirituality

The psychoanalyst Neville Symington (Ward 1993: 50) writes about natural religions and revealed religions, placing psychoanalysis in the former category. If we are part of a religious tradition that focuses on revelation, such as Christianity, Judaism or Islam, it is possible that we fail to hear the genuine spiritual search of someone we are listening to, because they are not expressing it in the terms with which we are familiar. There is a significant counselling approach known as 'transpersonal', based on aspects of Jungian psychology (Perry 1991) and on the work of Assagioli (Whitmore 2000), Wilber (Rowan 1983: 131ff.), Rowan (1983) and others, all of whom recognize the spiritual dimension as essential. Counsellors from other traditions, such as psychodynamic counselling, also acknowledge this vital spiritual dimension. Jacobs writes of 'living illusions' (1993b) and I have described 'psychodynamic theology' (Ross 1997). Sperry (2001) helpfully explores how to incorporate the spiritual dimension into psychotherapy and counselling, as does Thorne (1998) who explores the spiritual dimension from a person-centred perspective. Rowan (1983: 33) writes,

> A client is a spiritual being on a spiritual path (even though they may not be aware of it yet) and some of the material they bring is at that level. Jung showed long ago how dreams might reveal spiritual directions and spiritual longings which could be quite surprising to the person at a conscious level. Unless we are listening for these things, we are quite likely to miss them.

In a predominately secular world where most people do not belong to any religious grouping there is still a huge spiritual hunger that sometimes finds expression in counselling or in popular culture.

The social and the political

My initial training in counselling was through leading group therapy with psychiatric patients. This 'on the job' training opened a whole new world. In that world, with its context of people experiencing mental health problems, social isolation, stigma and prejudice, I came to see that the nature of counselling includes political and social dimensions. What was the purpose of a patient experiencing a cathartic release through group experience if he had no place to go when his health recovered? Politicians speak glibly of care in the community but show little commitment to funding the necessary changes. Meeting the needs of people requires wider listening to their context, especially to the social and political issues that affect them. Lago and Thompson (1996: 7–8, 14) in *Race, Culture and Counselling* touch on the broader social issues:

> The climate ... is a profoundly complex one in terms of history, population complexity, political perspectives and a huge range of cultural identities. All this is further compounded by discrimination and racism. Both counsellors and clients are participants in this climate, and as such, are subject to a multitude of complex forces and attitudes that shape people's lives. The contents alone indicate that any overly simplistic assumptions about the nature of British society and the people who live in it just cannot be made. Counsellors and psychotherapists have to acknowledge that their assumptions and beliefs about and attitudes towards those who are culturally and racially different may well be, oversimplistic, judgmental and discriminatory.

Jill began work as a counsellor in a racially diverse university setting, which she found enormously challenging. Over time she learnt a great deal from ethnically different clients. While she was not aware of being judgemental and discriminatory, on reflection she felt she had been over-simplistic at the start. It had not occurred to her that she was 'white' and all that this implied for herself and her non-white clients. Reflecting on this she could begin to see how race and colour needed to be owned before it could be addressed. Now she finds racial diversity the most rewarding element of her job.

In pastoral care, as in counselling, the helper has opportunities to work with people wherever they are and wherever they have come from. Counselling skills could be widely used, cutting across class, economic and racial barriers and having a radical impact on society. There are vital links with spirituality as well. 'A communally shared spirituality encourages the development of a free society, because societal understanding feeds naturally into political legislation, social action and personal responsibility' (Hay 2001: 11).

So listening is much more complicated and challenging than might at first be assumed. The stereotype of pastoral listening ('More tea, vicar?') could not be further from the truth. The ability to hear what people are actually saying and to acknowledge their feelings; recognition that part of being themselves is also located physically in the body; awareness of issues around gender and sexuality, spirituality and the social and political dimensions – all these produce a rich appreciation of the value and complexity of the individual. Such an appreciation finds its parallel in each religious tradition, expressed, for example, in Judaeo-Christian terms as being made in the image of God, as well as in the belief in the God who listens.

2 Active listening, using reflecting back and paraphrasing

What I have described up this point is passive listening; our task has been to enable the other person to speak. A new level is engaged when the pastoral carer begins to use active listening skills, which are less common in social conversation. Jacobs's book of facilitating skills, *Swift to Hear* (2000), includes a range of practical exercises. Here I highlight some of the key skills.

• Reflect back what the person says at a verbal level. One helpful exercise is done in pairs. One person talks for three minutes about something that has happened to him/her recently. His/her partner listens. Then the listener reflects back what the speaker has said. Obviously listeners are not going to be able to recall every word, but, as with skimming a newspaper, they should be able to recall the headlines. This seems artificial at first, but once tried it is exciting to discover just how much can be recalled when concentrating on listening. I had a difficult pastoral encounter with a church leader who felt he had been passed over for a post that he thought was his. As we talked I simply recounted the huge list of activities in which he was already engaged. He looked at me suspiciously and said 'Who told you that?' The answer was simple – he had, in a previous conversation. His suspicion turned to amazement and then self-respect because someone had actually listened to him. He needed someone to recognize the very valuable work he was already doing.

- Reflect back what the person says at a feeling level. Try the same exercise as before only this time swap roles. Note the body language and feed back after another three minutes the feelings that have been communicated, verbally and non-verbally. This may bring some surprises. Observation of feelings often enables people to feel they have been listened to at greater depth. Avoid adding interpretations or asking questions at this stage. When observation of feelings conflicts with what the person is saying, studies have shown that it is the non-verbal cues that are a more reliable indicator (Hetherington 2001).

- Paraphrase what the person says. This is the next step after reflecting back, offering a summary of what the person has been saying as a way of showing that you have heard and understood. What people think they have said is not always what the listener has heard and this allows them the opportunity to change or add details, or correct wrong impressions. This is a more difficult skill than it sounds. The desire to correct (even unconsciously) what the person is saying is deep-rooted, especially if it is something the helper feels uncomfortable about. Another temptation is to lead the person in a certain direction rather than following their lead.

Steve: I wanted to talk to you because I think you will understand. I've tried talking to the minister but it's no good, he just doesn't listen. I like him but he's so keen on evangelism that whatever I say always comes back to that subject and evangelism is the last thing I want to do at the moment. I'm not sure what I believe any more, so talking to others about God is not for me.

Counsellor: You are talking to me because I don't have the same agenda as your minister and will listen to you, whatever you believe.

Steve: I really doubt that God is interested in me. I feel so worthless. It's been going on for the last year and I feel such a fraud. I live in two worlds, church and work and I feel torn in two. I can't go on like this . . . [looks sad]

> *Counsellor*: I hear sadness and feelings of worthlessness where you feel you let everyone down and it is tearing you apart.

Paraphrasing enables the listener to get into the life of the client and make vital points of connection.

- Use questions to clarify. One of the vital functions of counselling skills is to help someone tell their story. When a story is being told for the first time it may be confused or incomplete. People do not always provide a neat beginning, middle and end to their narratives. The listener can hold the fragmented story so that the person can work out where he or she is in it. The use of appropriate questions can help this. However, we must avoid allowing our natural curiosity to lead us to ask more and more, especially if the subject is sensational or powerful. The purpose of a question is to clarify what is helpful, and should not leave the person feeling unheard.

> Jinney's father committed suicide. Several friends called to help in her time of grief, and the minister visited and helped with the funeral arrangements. Months later Jinney began talking to a pastoral carer in her faith community about her anger with her friends. At one point she turned to him and cried 'Do you know what they really wanted? Those so-called friends? They wanted to know how he did it and I didn't want to tell them. Why should anyone know? I felt under so much pressure but there is a stubborn bit in me that wouldn't give in. Now I feel so cool towards them; I love them and I hate them.'

This use of questions is a delicate balance guided by the important principle that the story being told is of the utmost importance. It is a story that has been waiting to be told and it needs to be told in that person's own way, with minimal intrusion. The purpose of questions is to prompt rather than obstruct the flow with unnecessary detail that is primarily for our benefit.

- Creative challenge. Another way of helping people is to encourage them to take responsibility for their own thoughts and behaviour. Sometimes they are looking for someone who will sympathize but not help them to change, or who will sort their problem out for them. Empathy is important, but so is challenging people to look at themselves. Being asked for our opinion is flattering, but it is better to encourage someone to challenge his or her own thinking. And sometimes we may have to confront what we feel to be unacceptable behaviour: Susie Orbach gives an example, where she felt she had to challenge the lying of a client. At first she was uncertain about doing this but felt that unless she did she was not being true to her own professional standards (1999: 40–1). Any challenge needs to be made creatively and sensitively, since religious people are especially prone to experiencing guilt and feelings of being judged. Judgemental phrases, criticism or harsh application of religious beliefs, even unspoken disapproval, can wreck a fragile pastoral relationship. On the other hand, avoiding the area of faith may be colluding in some way, as if religious belief and practice are a no-go area.

3 Making connections: 'it seems as if . . .'

When working with people in a faith community it is often valuable to connect what is going on in them with the religious beliefs they hold. A particular problem for faith communities is that they are potentially an escape or refuge from the world outside.

> By a devout commitment to celebrating key Jewish festivals, Fishel was able to hold down the uncomfortable feelings inside that he did not matter to anyone. As long as he belonged to family, friends and synagogue he felt all right. But his desire for a partner became more and more of a problem – no one in his circle was ever quite right. Eventually after going on sick leave because of stress he went to a Jewish counsellor. Before long his counsellor said to him 'Fishel, as you have been talking about the stress at work and feeling isolated in the office, taking all the responsibility, it seems as if you are telling me that it is hard for you to be on your own, not just at work.' The counsellor had made the connection for Fishel based on the limited information he had, and was able to offer it back to him. Fishel responded 'I never thought about it

> that way before, but it is true. I so long for a partner, a wife to share life with me.'

This making of connections is a four-way process. First, it links what is going on to the person's outer world – the 'real' world they live in most of the time. Secondly, it links with an inner world, replete with emotion and instinct, as well as the good and bad aspects of self and others. Thirdly, there is a link with the past and the difficult balance of meeting conflicting needs, helped or hindered by internal voices from the past. Fourthly, there are the vital links with the faith context and religious tradition. Life is never simple and there may be aspects of these strands that merge in a way that can be profoundly helpful or unhelpful.

> James was a student at university who became involved with a charismatic group belonging to the house church movement. He went from being an outgoing, carefree student to someone dogged by anxiety. He saw a counsellor at the student counselling service even though the leaders in his church had told him that what he really needed was more prayer. As the counsellor listened to James's story he helped him make connections between a powerful bullying father and what James felt was a powerful bullying God. Everything would be fine, he thought, as long as he did what the leaders told him to do; and so he would be the perfect Christian who would please God. It took some time for James to see that God was very different from his father and that he couldn't be the perfect Christian. He came to see that he could be a 'good enough' Christian, and made links with a group of other Christian students that met at the university.

4 Containing or bracketing our external frame of reference

Just as the counsellors made connections that helped Fishel and James in the examples above, there are times when it may be appropriate, while acknowledging the faith context, not to let it intrude into the caring relationship of the moment. Nobody likes failure or letting others down, yet it happens. When it does, the last thing we want is to be reminded of failure. The pain of our psyche longs for an understanding word or a human connection. The wounded spirit is unbearably sensitive.

Jan talked about her feelings about having an affair. Andy listened, aware of the various levels described in this chapter. As a person of faith Andy knew that what Jan had done had broken a biblical commandment. Jan knew this too, but in the next forty minutes of their encounter Andy did not raise this subject; instead he focused on her pain. Was this a collusive act, pretending that nothing had happened? Andy felt that it was neither the time nor the place for him to introduce the religious dimension. His focus was that the hurting person in front of him was of the utmost importance. Several years later they met accidentally after Jan had moved to another part of the country, and had apparently given up her religious belief. Jan described to Andy how accepting the encounter had been and that it provided her with a memory of healing, so that whatever else happened, she felt she had been heard and understood. Another year after this Jan got in contact with Andy again and talked about a new sense of faith, one which she felt able to express actively for the first time in many years. Andy had helped by containing Jan's pain and holding the external religious belief system in a way that nurtured rather than attacked Jan at a time of distress and vulnerability, both initially, and when he met her later. This does not mean that Andy gave up on his own belief or felt that it did not matter; but he dealt with it in a respectful way.

All these counselling skills are important and, like those described in later chapters, can be developed in further training, such as a counselling or counselling skills course. But no matter how good a person's skills, they must be matched by relational qualities, and it is these, especially in relation to the initial stage of pastoral care, that I examine in the next chapter.

Chapter 5

Starting out – the initial stage of pastoral skills

Relational qualities

Relationships have always played a vital part in religious tradition and faith communities, from the earliest relationship of God with Abraham, asking him to go out in faith to a land he did not yet know. With the key Christian focus on the crucial need for a relationship with God, made possible by the life, death and resurrection of Jesus Christ, there is another crucial emphasis on relationship. This emphasis on relationship has also been expressed in counselling and psychotherapy. Peter Lomas, a creative thinker and teacher of psychotherapy writes,

> Although crucially influenced by Freud – for it is he who has picked us up and placed us on the path of psychotherapy – I find I am deeply and consistently moved by a desire to emphasize, in a way that psychoanalysis does not, the intrinsic worth of personal relationships ... Thus, the relationship between the therapist and the patient will be valuable in its own right.
>
> (1993: 3)

The relational qualities that are essential to the use of counselling skills in this initial stage can be described as follows.

1 Being real and concrete

Being concrete is a way of enabling people to be specific about what it is they are saying or feeling. Sometimes we need to put into words what we feel the other person is saying and feeling, such as 'Are you saying to me that the news shocked you?' When we have listened well to somebody, we can help them focus, through hearing their own words back from us, so that they can see their situation with clarity. Often an issue that someone has been reflecting on for some time becomes real to them when they express it to others through words or feelings. The best way of enabling others to be real and concrete in their perception is to be the same ourselves.

2 Being present and immediate

Most of us have experienced trying to listen to someone who drives us to distraction. One person talks incessantly about a subject, which he has told the listener about many times before; another is so demanding that the listener feels utterly drained by the end of the conversation. It is difficult to be fully present with all people all the time, but we need to find a way of doing so if we are to help them. I can still recall tutors at theological college who communicated non-verbally in powerful ways that they wished I did not have a pressing question and that they really wanted to be elsewhere. It would have been more helpful if they had been real with me, explaining that I had not chosen the best moment. In that way I would have known that they were present with me and engaged with what I wanted to ask of them, even if it had to be at another time. In a counselling context immediacy means staying with the person in focus, in the actual conversation as it is happening. It requires a degree of engagement that precludes wandering off into other thought processes. Immediacy is often communicated through non-verbal signals such as eye contact, tone of voice, and the way the helper is sitting, all making for a sense of engagement, or, when absent, conveying relational distance.

3 Expressing acceptance and empathy

Another way in which people learn to trust others is through the sense of being really heard and accepted. In an exercise with a group of students on a counselling skills course, I asked them to write down the times when they had been rejected. Most students could recall in detail such events, some of which went back twenty or thirty years. The pain of those rejections was all too evident; it had left real psychological scars. So we worked on how, when it came to forming a helping relationship, we could overcome the unspoken rejection that most people carry around with them as part of their psychological 'baggage'. Acceptance was seen to be a vital capacity. But the question often arises in religious circles: 'How can you accept someone who is doing something that is wrong?' As caring people we may see others as flawed (as we all are in various ways) but we also need to see people as hurt, as real and human, and who are just as valued as anyone else. Empathy, a concept commonly used in counselling, is an expression of the further development of acceptance. Carl Rogers, who first stressed the importance of the term, defined it as

> entering into the private perceptual world of the other and becoming thoroughly at home in it. It involves being sensitive, moment by moment, to the changing felt meanings which flow in this other person, to the fear or rage or tenderness or confusion or whatever that he or she is experiencing. It means temporarily living in the other's life, moving about in it delicately without making judgements.
>
> (1980: 142)

This is no easy task. It requires the person offering care to become familiar with themselves through self-awareness. It is difficult to move delicately through another's pain without having encountered one's own. Within faith traditions with prescribed beliefs, empathy poses particular challenges, because people are not usually what they appear, and inevitably do not live up to what they believe. There can be a conflict of beliefs and values – Chapter 12 – yet the life of faith has to hold belief and doubt, hope and fear in tension, and work out a relationship that acknowledges all this. The challenge to be empathic in a faith context involves a willingness to hold beliefs more loosely and risk journeying into an unknown landscape. Egan (1994: 105ff.) provides a helpful exploration of empathy with a series of examples that demonstrate how this skill can be developed. It is a total hearing of the other, which paradoxically involves all of us and yet requires us to remain separate. As we listen our thinking is stimulated, our emotions are stirred, our body reacts, our imagination expands, our unconscious is awakened (even if we are not always aware of it) and our spirit is touched; and yet all this experience is contained (so as not to swamp empathy for the other with our own story). Empathy is a dynamic occurrence both for the person and the helper, so that the empathic 'experience of knowing another is one of mystery and grace' (Kornfeld 1998: 56). It provides a radical demonstration of the acceptance of God in Christian terms, or being a valued part of a community in Jewish terms.

One danger is that empathy can be such a powerful experience that there is a temptation to merge with the other person's experience and lose objectivity or even identity. Wright (1991: 141) describes it this way. 'So if I am to know by identification, there must be a sense in which I take with me, into the identification, the thin, fine line of difference, of separation, that preserves for me the objectness of the Other and the space for thought.'

4 Self-awareness

As we recognize the need for these basic qualities, we must also recognize some basic barriers that hinder the use of counselling skills in a pastoral context. One way of recognizing what these barriers may be is to become more aware of what goes on in us, and in our relationships with others. I have already referred several times to the importance of self-awareness, and this is a necessary preparation for entering into any helping relationship. But awareness also includes the following.

Our past history

One of the crucial differences between the pastoral task and other helping relationships is that there is usually a history to the relationship. If both parties are members of a faith community, there is likely to have been contact in the past: sharing in worship; discussing issues of policy; attending social functions; having friends in common; choosing future religious leaders; disagreeing with the other's decisions; attending the same committee meetings and so on. Belonging to the same group also means there is something in common in faith terms. Our previous history with a person can be both a help and a hindrance. It may help us to establish a rapport based on shared connections, to see patterns in the person's life based on a wider perspective, to establish continuity in an ongoing relationship beyond the present helping aspect; and it can speed up the process of listening because some things do not need to be said: they can be safely assumed.

But history is a hindrance in that sometimes these assumptions are wrong. People in the same community may hold different beliefs, or may react to the same experience very differently. A crucial part of the pastoral task is to check out, by listening carefully to people, what it is that they mean, so as not to jump to unwarranted conclusions. In addition to this, if the carer has a particular role, such as a priest or rabbi, people may respond in a certain way. They may not tell the whole story for fear of being judged by someone who is an authority figure. They may disagree about the direction the minister wants to take the faith community. They may resent the minister's presence, preferring a more traditional predecessor. It is this difficulty that leads me to emphasize that people who do not have a formal religious role or title can often offer much the best listening in church and faith communities.

Our personal motives

A pastoral relationship can all too often be used as a surrogate experience to meet our own needs. Whilst we all have needs and are in relationships that often have ambivalent feelings involved in them, we need to meet our own needs and examine our relationships through our own personal counselling, experiential growth or professional supervision, and not vicariously through the act of pastoral care. Our purpose in pastoral care is to help the other person, not to try and resolve our own difficulties.

Our need to rescue

Another motive found in faith traditions is the need to rescue people; to 'save' them. This evangelistic imperative is a feature of different faith traditions that seek to convert others to their religious beliefs. There are numerous well-meaning groups in all religions that seek the salvation of others. Within the pastoral care context there will always be a tendency to want to impose a belief system on others, even if it does not go so far as believing that the real work of pastoral care is to save the person's soul. Some forms of so-called Christian counselling come under this banner (Bond 1993: 73). The subtle difference is that they see the essential problem a person has as a spiritual one, and until this is resolved they do not think all the pastoral care in the world will ultimately help. John Diamond, the journalist who died of throat cancer, wrote poignantly about his experiences. After telling the world through a national newspaper column about his cancer, he was surprised at the response.

> I have now received every tract, leaflet, edition of the Bible and holy relic known to the main Christian churches in Britain. I think I know all the arguments there are for putting my trust in Jesus. I thank you for passing on the good word on to me, and know this is something you feel you must do. I thank you, too, for all your prayers at sundry churches, temples, cathedrals and sites of pilgrimage. I remain, however, a secular Jew. I imagine I'll be that way for good now.
>
> (*The Times* Magazine, 13 March 1999)

What he experienced was a very human response to help, to care, to do something. Yet as Diamond gently points out, he had made his own decisions and he lived and died with them as best he could. The desire to rescue others is both exemplary and dangerous. Care and compassion for others is a hallmark of, although not exclusive to, religious traditions, and it would be surprising if it were not expressed in faith communities. The danger lies in letting the desire to rescue overwhelm the needs or desires of the other person to such an extent that something is forced on them that they do not want.

Other counsellors and pastoral carers are Christians who work professionally and do not impose a worldview on the people they help. They may feel embarrassed at being identified with more fundamentalist groups (Ross 2001). Yet the need to rescue is a powerful psychological, not just spiritual, drive in many people. A common feature in those beginning counselling skills training is the desire to help others. At one level this is both laudable and essential, although counsellors have to learn that helping does not mean trying to 'sort out' the client.

The worst expressions of pastoral care occur when helpers override the needs of the individual and leave the person feeling worse. There is no real meeting or relationship, and this of course then reflects upon the faith community from which the help is offered. Self-awareness is a vital part of the task of preparation, and this in turn will stimulate a journey of personal growth. As we learn more about being comfortable and whole with ourselves we will in turn have more resources to offer to others.

Chapters 3 to 5 have focused on the initial stages of the use of counselling skills that can be used within faith communities. Helping skills are used to accomplish a number of key tasks that include building the foundations of a trusting and accepting relationship, which allows the range of a person's experience to be heard and encountered. Chapters 6 to 8 take the model a stage further, describing the middle or intermediate stage of pastoral care, using skills, developing personal qualities and promoting the tasks that take people deeper into the questions and issues that trouble them.

Chapter 6

Moving on – the intermediate stage of pastoral skills

Tasks

One distinctive feature of working in a pastoral context is the diversity in the shape of its boundaries. Whilst researching this book I interviewed clergy across all the major Christian denominations, rabbis and others from the Jewish faith, pastoral counsellors, theologians, new age practitioners and others who, if not identifiable in these ways, still hold spirituality as a vital part of their being and counselling practice. Their responses were enormously diverse, although there was a consensus on certain key issues. One feature was the brevity in a pastoral context of most contacts with individuals. For example, a key pastoral issue in inner city Edinburgh is homelessness. Before the end of almost every church service someone is there asking for help – bringing with them other issues such as alcoholism and drugs. In this case the skills best used are those examined in the earlier chapters. At the other extreme was a Church of Scotland minister from the Highlands who did not understand the concept of pastoral care. In his village if there was an issue someone would tell him, and he would visit 'as the minister. That's what they expect me to do.' In contrast to the situation in Edinburgh, pastoral care was seen as a longer term relationship built up over years and sometimes generations.

This intermediate phase in this integrative helping relationship model focuses on the tasks, skills and relational qualities that enable a helping relationship to develop to greater depth over a period of time. Chapters 7 and 8 explore the relevant skills and relational qualities but, as in the initial phase, this chapter examines the particular tasks of the intermediate stage.

Helping skills: a relational approach	*Moving on – the intermediate stage*	
Tasks	1	Maintaining and developing the helping relationship
	2	Overcoming resistance to change
	3	Working on the problems or issues
	4	Facilitating new perspectives
	5	Linking past and present
	6	Maintaining boundaries
	7	Discovering new aspects of personal and emotional narrative
Skills	1	Communicating 'core values'
	2	Employing perceptive immediacy
	3	Using metaphors or simple interpretations
	4	Using challenge or confrontation in a way that enables progress
Relational qualities	1	Staying with the person, especially when they get 'stuck'
	2	Avoiding taking responsibility for the client
	3	Expressing non-possessive warmth

Certain tasks must be achieved if the use of counselling skills in a faith community is to enhance the life of the individual as well as the community. I have already stressed that the relationship between the helper and the person being helped is of crucial significance. The quality of the initial encounter determines whether the person wants to return. Coltart talks about patients seeing a psychoanalyst for the first time:

> I know from long experience that the patient never forgets a consultation. The details of the exchange fade, but the patient always remembers the overall feeling-tone of the meeting, the sense of comfort or discomfort, the colouring,

which renders it unique in his life . . . even as we open the door to the patient we are embarking on an event which will be uniquely memorable for him.

(1993: 70)

But the intermediate stage of the pastoral encounter, whether it is pastoral counselling or pastoral care, suggests several more tasks that sustain the relationship.

1 Maintaining and developing the helping relationship

Assuming that a good foundation has been laid, one important question is whether or not the person has the resources to work at a new and more demanding level with the pastoral carer. Some assessment is needed to see if the person can work in a psychological way in the pastoral context. The following considerations are important in assessing how helpful it might be to pursue the pastoral contact using counselling skills adapted from Coltart (1993: 72). The person should have

- an awareness that there is a psychological aspect of being that includes the conscious and the unconscious, not just the rational and theological;
- the ability to give a self-aware history, though not necessarily in chronological order;
- some emotional connection to his or her history;
- the ability to recall feelings and memories;
- the ability to step back and reflect on his or her story from a psychological and faith perspective;
- signs of a willingness to take responsibility for him/herself;
- the ability to use the imagination and understand metaphors and interpretations;
- a realistic level of self-esteem and a willingness to hope;
- a sense that the developing relationship with the helper is a comfortable one.

The absence of these does not negate the pastoral caring nature of a relationship, but may serve to highlight the limitations of what a person is able to take from that relationship at that time.

Neither are we looking only to work with people who fulfil all the criteria: they probably do not need much help! However 'it is perfectly possible for a person to come across as being intelligent, sophisticated, capable of sustained thought, aware of symptoms – and yet absolutely not psychologically-minded' (Coltart 1993: 72).

Jerry had come for counselling to Margaret, who was a Christian. The initial session did not include the use of a checklist as above. Despite an initial good start, she found it increasingly difficult to work with him because he was always avoiding the area of his feelings. He had many rational thought processes and varying degrees of guilt that left her feeling a failure every time he left. Her supervisor helped Margaret to see that what she was feeling was the 'failure' that was at the heart of Jerry's problem, and of which he was frightened. Margaret tried to introduce this into the counselling but found that it was very hard to establish any real rapport. After the third session Jerry announced that he was finishing counselling, as he could not afford it, and he left. Jerry's problems were complex and he was using some defence mechanisms that I examine below. However, looking at the checklist indicates that Jerry was probably unaware of a whole emotional dimension. Rather than force this on him, the right pastoral response was to work at the level that was best for him at that time. Jerry may simply have needed to tell his story and be heard. If he had felt heard he might then have been able to return at another time when he was ready to take things a little further.

---

2 Overcoming resistance to change

People are more likely to come for help at a time of crisis than at any other time. Out of the work done in this crisis, a pastoral bond may be formed, which can help powerfully in the future as well as for the present. The ongoing task in a faith community is to work with relationships, even when the person is reluctant to change. Many people find change uncomfortable and, indeed, sometimes the appeal of a faith community is that it is not expected to change. In a frenetic world where change is increasingly rapid it is comforting to be part of a community that seems to offer a safe haven from the disruption of life all around.

McBride (quoted in Sperry 2001: 81), writing from an American context, identifies how a life crisis can have a spiritual dimension, and lists common examples. These are:

- trauma;
- relationships and family problems;
- disillusionment with the Church [or faith community];
- belief transition;
- denominational identity;
- losses;
- physical illness;
- extremes of thinking or living;
- psychological disturbance;
- religious burnout;
- ethics conflict;
- personal identity;
- the crisis of working with people in crisis.

While some of these issues are dealt with in later chapters, their relevance here is that times of crisis and transition are often accompanied by questions about people's belief systems as they impact on their own living. These questions can generate enormous anxiety. People threatened by change or trauma may adopt what have been called defence mechanisms. These are psychological means of coping with threat – stress, anxiety or overwhelming feelings, which we fear will harm us. Defences are not erected consciously or deliberately and they are in fact important ways of protecting the self. 'All humans need to employ effective defences ... for survival ... For example, denial of illness is a normal life-preserving mechanism in the dying ... all humans are simply human. None of us copes effectively all the time' (Pattison 1990: 269). So the use of defences can be positive as well as negative (Coate 1989: 66).

The commonly identified defences are: denial; repression; rationalization; intellectualization; isolation; regression; fixation; idealization; splitting or dissociation; projection; introjection; displacement; reaction formation; asceticism; undoing; identification; and compensation (McLemore 1990: 319 ff.). The 'value in using these terms ... is to provide a shorthand language for communication ... to increase counsellors' awareness of the different strategies which people generally . . . adopt to avoid acknowledging what seems to them painful feelings and thoughts' (Jacobs 1988: 79 ff.). But there are two dangers to be avoided in using the language of defences: seeing them as 'labels', which appear to sum up people and their problems; and the belief that they need to be removed in order to get at the real problem. The key issue remains the quality of the relationship between the pastoral helper using counselling skills and the person in need. A positive helping relationship allows the person to lower his or her defences when it feels appropriate. Sometimes a helper may explain how a defence appears to be used, allowing the client the opportunity to see whether it might be safe enough to put the defence to one side.

Particular attention is needed when the defences we have mentioned are associated with aspects of religious beliefs and faith community structures. Jacobs identifies six areas of concern that can be encountered in pastoral practice, to which I add one of my own.

First, the use of rituals or words in obsessive ways. Ritual can be powerfully healing whether it is traditional, or a contemporary and relevant form. But ritual can also be just as powerful in generating anxiety, if people believe rituals have to be performed in particular ways. Unless the exact words are said with precisely correct actions, some people are overwhelmed by the anxiety about chaos or disorder welling up within. Behind this may lie a view of a God who punishes, resulting from an upbringing in which the child learned to gain approval by having to do things the 'right' way. For example, a church member accosted a new assistant minister after a service in which a free-form style of worship was introduced. This lay leader shook with anger, as he demanded to know by what right the minister had changed 'a perfectly good and proper way of doing things'. Thomas Merton, a great twentieth-century mystic, was well aware of this danger when he suggested that even the liturgical life can become a hiding place producing men and women 'who go through a pantomime of perfection quite unaware of their spiritual mediocrity and of their being in reality loveless casualties' (Merton 1973: 9).

Second, the use of a sacred text, such as the Bible or the Koran, in a way that cannot be challenged or discussed. So much authority is given to the divine authorship that any questioning of this is met with 'horror and extreme defensiveness' (Jacobs 1993a: 175). This often goes hand in hand with a reaction against intellectual growth. As a chapter in one book expresses it, 'What good is psychology if the Bible tells us all we need to know?' (Collins 1988a: 93). This defence against the anxiety of challenging an ultimate authority is also found in various forms of Christian counselling that use the Bible as a means of exhorting a person to change in a particular spiritual direction (CWR 1996). Or some people look for a text to justify what they want to do.

One young person, Gina, told her minister that God was calling her to work in Israel because every time she opened the Bible, there was the word 'Israel'. Despite advice to the contrary she eventually went to Israel as a missionary, but stayed only a little over six months. The reality was that this was the only acceptable escape from an intolerable family situation. Gina discovered that we often take our histories with us, and her family dominated her thinking and feeling as much in Israel as they did at home. On her return home she sought professional help, and was able to face the complexity and pain of the family and to see what had made her use the Bible in this way.

Third, rationalization can be used to disguise unconscious fears. By rationalization I mean a rational, logical reason employed to account for a certain action or opinion. Sometimes these 'rationalizations' are a way of covering inner fear or anxiety. Jacobs refers to the ordination of women in the Church of England as an example, where intellectual reasons against ordination of women may mask discomfort at having to deal more equally with women. Every religious tradition has its fears but, while they need to be recognized and owned, it is sometimes harder to detect the fear behind the rationalization of the person you are trying to help.

Andrew was the unappointed guardian of the church rule book, reinforced by his occupation as a solicitor. He would speak up at meetings about the need to maintain heritage and tradition and quote the relevant clauses. If ever there was any move to change, Andrew appeared as an ever-present obstacle. However, a chance conversation with an older member added new insight. Andrew had once been the youth leader and tried to bring about many changes. At a meeting he had been humiliated by an older member who was virulently opposed to any change. It appeared that Andrew had been deeply hurt by this experience, and was afraid of this happening again. He was protecting himself with the rule book, even if he was in danger of becoming like the person that had hurt him.

Fourth, any religious group can project on to God or other religious figures whatever they want to do themselves. Using fundamentalist language and depicting the enemy as the Devil enables some religious groups to justify mounting terrorist attacks in a so-called holy war. History is littered with illustrations of this use of God to justify political and military ends. The Crusades, the establishment of the Church of England, the persecution of Jews, the colonization of Africa, and the slave trade are but a few examples. This is most likely to be experienced in pastoral practice when someone is troubled by mental health problems. 'God has told me to stop taking this medication as He is going to heal me' said a man with manic depression. It can be very difficult to help people withdraw their projections and look more closely at themselves.

Fifth, prayer can be seen as a 'quick fix', but in reality can be a way of avoiding difficult relationships, intrusive thoughts and uncomfortable feelings. Prayer can of course be a moment of profound intimacy with God, or even involve a sense of desolation in a place of darkness. Yet prayer can be treated lightly as if it is a helpline to a celestial breakdown repair service. Merton counters this view when he writes,

> We should let ourselves be brought naked and defenceless into the centre of dread where we stand alone before God in our nothingness without explanation, without theories, completely dependent upon his providential care, in dire need of his gift of grace, his mercy, and the light of faith . . . True contemplation is not a psychological trick but a theological grace.
>
> (Merton 1973: 13)

This form of prayer is a way of taking real responsibility for who we are and what we do.

Sixth, Merton's monastic contributions raise the whole question of sublimation, especially in the area of sexuality. By sublimation I mean the way we substitute one thought or activity with another that is more culturally, socially or religiously acceptable. So the old comment made to young men, 'Go and have a cold shower', suggested an activity that sublimated their sexual desire. Different religious traditions use sublimation as a defence against fear of sexual thought and feelings. It may be expressed for some people through their vows of celibacy or chastity. But other 'unacceptable' feelings are often sublimated, including anger. Many Christian clients have real difficulty with acknowledging and expressing anger so they sublimate it through passive aggression (such as the silent saboteur who 'innocently' undermines the pastor's best ideas), unaware that they are having a damaging impact on the life of the community.

Seventh, the personal experience or conversion process itself can become a religious defence. Conversion is a real and important part of religious traditions and has an authentic role within such faith communities. However, it still can be used defensively.

Keith became a Christian very suddenly. He felt his life was in a mess, he was feeling depressed, his marriage had broken down and he was at a point of despair. A friend invited him to church where, for the first time, he felt he belonged, and over a few weeks made a specific commitment to become a Christian. Life was suddenly wonderful and Keith began to tell everybody about why they should become Christians too. His enthusiasm, at first embarrassing, gradually became obsessive. Then Keith crashed, and his world fell around him just as it had threatened to do before. The pastoral carer, who had been helping Keith, helped him over a period of time to see that his faith needed to be based in real life, not as an escape from life with all its ambiguities and pain.

Understanding how religion can be used defensively is a first step. We must also recognize that such defences are often difficult to shift; the pastoral helper can only draw attention to them, and in a non-judgemental way. The key factor for change is a pastoral relationship in which there can be created 'a sense of trust which enables the barriers to be lowered, in order to allow the particular feelings and thoughts to come to the surface, where they can be expressed, accepted and a start made towards understanding them' (Jacobs 1993a: 174).

3 Working on the problems or issues

The problems that people bring are wide-ranging and often complex, as can be seen in the diversity of issues that provokes spiritual crises. The purpose of using counselling skills at this level is more than being a listening ear or an alternative to the Samaritans, valuable though both these are. The key role in this middle stage is helping the person and his or her story to move forward. This involves two crucial factors – the person being helped must actually want help, and must be willing to take responsibility for his or her own life. Some people complain about their situation but do not want to change. They value the time and attention that they are given by pastoral carers but are resistant to accepting that they have a part to play in making constructive moves to alter the way things are for them. Others simply want someone else to make things better for them, like a child expecting a parent to sort out its mess. Given that one criticism of faith communities is that they can be authoritarian and parental, it is understandable that people come wanting help and expecting it to be delivered in this way. Egan calls the end of the first stage of his helping model 'Client action: the heart of the helping process' (1994: 29). This requires clients to recognize their part, and implies that a pastoral relationship aided by counselling skills is quite different from, for example, a doctor–patient, lawyer–client model, where the professional knows best.

4 Facilitating new perspectives

As a person is able to tell his or her story and know that it is being heard, a new perspective may develop. Through the responses of the pastoral carer the person can begin to see and feel from a different vantage point: 'As you were telling your story I was struck by how matter of fact it seemed. Yet your voice conveyed a lot of feeling, so I wonder where those feelings are now?' As a child I recall coming to London for the first time and being in Piccadilly Circus in a huge crowd. All I could see was a forest of legs, until a policeman parted several adults and brought me to stand next to him. I discovered it was a royal premiere and saw an elegant Rolls Royce deliver the Queen on to red-carpeted pavement. My change of position and perspective transformed a confusing, jostled experience into a magical memory, which defines an aspect of my childhood. A new perspective, a new way of seeing and experiencing often facilitates the development of hope. Lyall writes, 'The task of the pastor is to help in the construction of hopeful future stories, of invoking within the imagination of someone in despair the possibility of seeing life differently' (2001: 105). Such pastoral conversations require a sensitivity of approach and careful timing.

Sarah sat next to the hospital bed where Gary lay in a coma after a car crash. Nobody knew if he would recover or if he would be brain-damaged. To offer to Sarah the glib promise that all would be well since Gary was in the hands of God (as had been said by a previous well-meaning visitor) would be a cruel mockery of sensitive pastoral care. All the minister was able to do was listen, which he did well. Gary made a recovery, albeit with some changes to his personality and with a more limited short-term memory. Sarah sat in the study and cried 'He's not the same Gary I knew; I want the old Gary back. I feel so awful even thinking this, I've never told anyone this before.' The minister listened and helped Sarah to see that there could be a different way of viewing the situation. He did this by using the resource of a shared faith tradition that gives to God a part in each life and the fulfilment of it. He reminded Sarah of God's perspective and his sense that God still had a part to play in the unfolding days ahead, though he could not guarantee what that would be. In some circumstances this might look as if Sarah was being 'preached' at, but it was in fact the pastoral sensitivity of this minister and his understanding of Sarah's frame of reference, including her faith in God, that were carefully held together. Her despair had turned into hope and she had seen the fulfilment of that in Gary's recovery. He had changed, but not to the extent that Sarah had feared. She needed a safe place to express these fears, and she could then recover for herself the recognition that she still loved Gary and that they would continue to have a future together.

5 Linking past and present

Kay had been having regular sessions with the vicar, Janet, during which, as Janet listened, Kay had begun to talk about her past. One day she was walking down the wood parquet floor just after it had been polished, leaving a distinctive smell, when she whirled round to Janet and said 'Who made you do that?' Janet was perplexed but before she could answer Kay stormed out of the door. She did not attend church that Sunday but did turn up for the next appointment. Kay was very angry and Janet enquired what this was about. 'It's that bloody floor! You did have to go and polish it, didn't you?', she shouted before lapsing into silence. Janet, who had trained in pastoral counselling, replied gently 'I wonder if there's ever been another floor like that?' Kay began to cry and told Janet for the first time about her past with a physically abusive mother who would make her polish the floor when she came home from school. Her mother would stand over her, as Kay was on her hands and knees, and if any part was not done meticulously to her satisfaction she would hit Kay with a hair brush across the back of the legs. Janet had used her training in linking the past with the present, commonly appreciated in psychodynamic counselling.

The pastoral carer is likely to make connections when listening to a person in need, though rarely as dramatically as in the last example. Such a task is more difficult than it first appears, since some people are resistant to allowing the past to carry any significance for them – sometimes, indeed, because it is so powerful that it has to be dismissed. Some religious people say 'The past is the past, my sins are forgiven.'

Seeing the past and linking it with the present was what most helped Keith overcome the defensiveness of his sudden conversion. He discovered that many of his problems were linked to his parents' divorce when he was a young child. He had never told anyone but he felt he was to blame. He tried to be a 'good boy' and longed for his father to return. His depression as an adult was also linked to the death of his father. He found in Christianity a Father God who would never let him down and he was still trying to be a 'good boy', to please the Almighty Father. Such an illusion was bound to fail. Through a pastoral relationship in which the helper was aware both of the spiritual content of his conversion experience and of the possible defences involved, Keith was able to discover a faith that was less idealized and much more real.

6 Maintaining boundaries

When we use the term boundary, the first image that may come to mind is the boundary round a cricket field, essential when it comes to scoring runs. But in a pastoral relationship boundaries, lines that should not be crossed, though also important, are often less clear than on the cricket field. In counselling, boundaries contain the development of a therapeutic relationship so that it does not slip into being something else. The client may bring unrealistic beliefs, expectations and needs to counselling, and attempt to draw the counsellor into the kind of dysfunctional relationship that may have contributed to the client's problem in the first place, or that is a continuing difficulty for the client (Trower *et al.* 1988: 36). For example, the client who wants the pastor to provide all the answers may try to draw him or her into answering a series of questions.

A key aspect of the pastoral relationship, and of using counselling skills in pastoral work, is that it is not formal counselling. Pastoral work rarely uses weekly, 50-minute sessions in the same place at the same time for a contracted period of time, working in accordance with a professional code of ethics and with a particular understanding of confidentiality. Some churches have developed codes of practice for pastoral care, which help delineate the necessary boundaries, since they are very important. The following checklist clarifies some of the issues.

- What is the existing relationship you have with the person?
- How frequently are you expecting to meet and where?
- Is meeting in a home situation, either yours or the other's, the best practice?
- What about confidentiality? Who is included and who is excluded?
- Is there a power imbalance, through a formal role in the faith community? If so, how will this be addressed?
- Is this expected to be an ongoing relationship or a more casual, occasional pastoral conversation?
- Do you feel attracted to the person or is it obvious they are attracted to you?
- Is there something about this person that you find difficult, challenging or threatening?
- Does the context of the faith community impose other restrictions appropriate to the beliefs and culture of the faith?
- If working with children, should another adult be present?
- Do you have a working knowledge of good practice in relation to abuse: physical, sexual or emotional?
- Is it clear that the responsibility for the work is that of the person being helped?
- How respectful are you of this person's belief system and his or her pastoral concerns?
- Where do you get the appropriate professional support for working as a pastoral helper using counselling skills? Is the person being helped secure enough if this supervision is part of the faith community?

This list is not exhaustive and can be extended by pastoral practitioners within their own faith context. It does demonstrate that the nature of pastoral relationships is currently viewed with increasing professionalism and rigour as regards what is and is not appropriate in using counselling skills in the pastoral context. There is still a tension to be faced, which Lyall expresses in this way.

> In the parish context, where much counselling begins within the informal structure of pastoral care, it can be

difficult to move to the formal contracts required for successful counselling. For one thing, such formalities as time-bound meetings may not be expected by the parishioner; for another, there already exists a possibly deeper kind of implicit pastoral contract between the minister and congregation: that the minister is constantly available for pastoral care, day and night – a contract which itself needs re-examining in many cases.

(1995: 62)

Lyall is addressing the limitations of the minister/member relationship; in theory pastoral carers who do not have a formal religious role should have more scope and should be able to use counselling skills in a less restrictive way. But the context is part of the issue and Lyall helpfully points out the dangers of a lack of boundaries. The other side to this issue is that while boundaries need to be maintained, they are not set in concrete: given the dynamic nature of relationships and the flexibility and tensions of a faith community structure, boundaries need careful attention as an ongoing aspect of engagement in professional pastoral care.

7 Discovering new aspects of personal and emotional narrative

Once Kay (see page 65) understood that her past had been very painful, she began to see how she resented people who lived in 'posh' houses with wooden floors. She recognized that the person she really resented, and was very angry with, was not Janet but her mother. With Janet's support Kay was able to write to her estranged mother, who replied recognizing her guilt and responsibility, in a manner that really helped. She in turn told Kay about some aspects of her own life, which enabled Kay to see her in a new light. This did not eradicate the pain and anger that Kay felt, but it allowed a new dimension of her emotional narrative to emerge. Kay also began to see that she had avoided relationships with women, which was something she wanted to change for the future.

This fresh discovery that comes though a personal and emotional narrative lies at the heart of Kogan's work (1995) with the sons and daughters of Holocaust survivors. Using psychoanalytic techniques that are more specialist than are traditionally found in pastoral care, Kogan is still able to focus on the place of narrative. She uses analytic terms, but the same process can be found in good pastoral care when the carer is open to the opportunity to let new life come into being.

> From the mute cry at the start, and along the continuation of the analytic process, through the ongoing intimate dialogue, a comprehensible narrative evolves. What emerges is a story of real events (for example, Isaac's father's story about the execution of his own father which he and his mother were witness to) . . . It is a narrative that emerges hauntingly in a newly-found analytic relationship . . . Both analyst and patient eagerly await the story which emerges from this quest . . . and thus allows life to be more whole.
>
> (1995: 160–1)

One of the enriching aspects of the good use of counselling skills is watching people cope with enormous issues from the past and make courageous decisions for the present and the future. The presence of hope is as refreshing as sunlight streaming into a darkened room and revealing its beauty. This possibility comes from the tasks outlined here. The intermediate stage of the pastoral encounter also benefits from further skills and personal qualities in the carer, which are discussed in the next two chapters.

Chapter 7

Moving on – the intermediate stage of pastoral skills

Skills

Although the counselling skills that are valuable in pastoral care can be learned, most people will already possess some of them, or recognize them in themselves in embryonic form. For the intermediate stage of pastoral care, most of those skills will need further development, which this chapter describes.

1 Communicating 'core values'

The term 'core values' is used by Culley (1991: 12ff.) to express aspects of Carl Rogers's 'core conditions' of unconditional positive regard, empathy and congruence. The focus here is on how the helping person expresses acceptance, understanding and authenticity as core values in the helping process. The challenge is to express all three aspects, which Mearns and Thorne sum up as 'to offer a relationship where the core conditions enable the client to feel understood, accepted and related to, as a real person, by a real person . . . when the client and counsellor enter deeply into relationship and, in Rogers' words, simply the presence of the therapist is "full of healing" ' (2000: 83). Rabbi Katz reflects further on this from a Jewish context:

> Rabbis and ministers would do well to inform themselves in a more organized way of the nature of empathy and to apply

this new conceptualization to their religious work. Contemporary psychology provides a new commentary on old religious texts and offers a new 'spiritual' discipline to qualify the rabbi to do 'practical theology' better. This is not a call for the clergy to rush to imitate the analyst, to surrender their own identity, or to neglect prayer, meditation, study of the Torah, or the practice of *mitzvoth* (commandments) . . . by adapting psychological principles to our own role we can enhance the effectiveness of our work . . . among the new techniques is empathic identification.

(1985:101ff.)

These core values can be an intrinsic part of a religious tradition; but the pastoral carer or helper needs, using a specifically theological word, to 'incarnate' these in the helping relationship. These values can be translated into particular ways of communicating, seen in the three new skills I introduce at this point.

2 Employing perceptive immediacy

Immediacy, as we saw in Chapter 5, means focusing on what the person is thinking and feeling at that moment, in the 'here and now'. It is hindered if the helper is busy thinking about problem solving, or appropriate religious advice or texts, rather than staying in the present moment with the person and his or her problem. But we can also fall into the trap of becoming preoccupied with the *problem*, especially if it is complex, and failing to stay with the person. At such a point a cognitive process has been substituted for immediacy. But in itself immediacy is not sufficient. It is an initial stage skill that needs further development. Immediacy involves a high degree of perceptiveness, or awareness of what the person is saying, not saying, or communicating through tone of voice and body language. Egan comments 'Your communications skills are only as good as the accuracy of the perceptions on which they are based' (1994: 108). If the perception we have of the person or their problem is wrong, it damages the helping process no matter how well we use our counselling skills. 'The kind of perceptiveness needed to be a good helper is based on the quality of one's being with clients and on practical intelligence. It is developed through experience' (Egan 1994: 108).

The development of perceptiveness is most often hindered by prejudices, or by making assumptions about someone, often in a stereotypical way. The equal opportunities policy statement of BACP (BACP 1998: 2) covers a full range of possible discrimination with

> due regard for those groups of people with identifiable char-
> acteristics which can lead to visible and invisible barriers
> thus inhibiting their joining and full participation in BACP.
> Barriers can include age, colour, creed, culture, disability,
> education, ethnicity, gender, information, knowledge,
> mobility, money, nationality, race, religion, sexual orienta-
> tion, social class and status.

The British Association for Counselling and Psychotherapy have recently published their *Ethical Framework for Good Practice in Counselling and Psychotherapy* (2002). Underpinning the issues they identify as vital for counselling and the use of counselling skills is a commitment to anti-discriminatory practice.

Faith communities provide examples of both good and bad practice in this area.

Wilma was a new pastoral worker in a London inner city church with an increasing black congregation. She began to visit families. Although not a trained counsellor, she was a good listener and as she went into the homes of black members they began to trust her and tell her what it was like coming to Brixton from the Caribbean in the 1950s. Wilma saw the pain as well as the tears in their eyes as they told their story of being rejected so many times by the church. Their resilient faith touched Wilma, who found she was apologizing on behalf of the church for the way these people of such real faith had been treated. This same church, during Wilma's time as pastoral assistant, sought to make amends for the past in welcoming a Ghanaian church to use their building; and subsequently developed strong links that demonstrated the vitality of faith across race, culture, age and gender.

3 Using metaphors or simple interpretations

The ability to work with metaphor is one of the indicators of a person who is psychologically minded and therefore better able to develop a pastoral relationship with greater therapeutic potential. Metaphors, similes or analogies are concrete concepts or images used to describe something more abstract, in this case how a person thinks and feels. The type of metaphor used in counselling might include 'I felt like one of those ducks on a lake: gracefully moving along on the surface, but madly scrabbling to make headway underneath.' Faith communities are rich in tradition and have particular metaphorical images that convey specific meanings. There are some lovely biblical metaphors which talk of God replacing a heart of stone with a heart of flesh (Ezekiel 36: 26); or phrases like 'wash me and I shall be whiter than snow' in David's moving psalm of confession (Psalm 51: 7). In counselling a metaphor can stand for a type of 'as if' statement. A pastoral carer may say in response to a client 'You are talking to me as if I were a priest hearing confession, wanting me to pronounce absolution.' People use metaphors and analogies to explain the feel of a situation or an event that they cannot put into exact words. 'I felt like I was a naughty schoolboy being called to see the Head', or 'Do you remember what it was like as a kid waking up in your room in the middle of the night, sure that something was there, being too frightened to open your eyes? That was what it felt like when . . .'. Often it is the person needing help who provides metaphors, which the helper can 'play' with or can expand upon, as a way of helping the other make sense of his or her experience, or acknowledge the emergence of issues which had previously been deeply hidden. One aspect of this is helping the person exchange 'petrified metaphors' and 'to share in creating moving metaphors which shift forward personal growth and open up new possibilities' (Hobson 1985: 59). Christians when going through difficult times commonly use metaphors drawn from the death of Jesus with images of abandonment, dereliction, crucifixion; but they may, with time and help, eventually replace these for themselves with images of resurrection.

The use of interpretation is a development of the empathic response, where the pastoral helper tries to link what he or she is hearing and feeling to what the client may be experiencing. 'As you have been talking about the school you work in and how it is falling apart at the seams, you sound as if you have been talking about yourself as you are here today' is one such interpretation. This type of response helps to effect a shift from the environment 'out there' that a person is talking about to the internal psychological environment that is being experienced in the pastoral relationship. Interpretation helps people understand and feel more of their narrative, and may enable them to construct a new narrative with a different meaning (McLeod 1998: 149). Jacobs views this as a more advanced skill that comes from the psychodynamic counselling tradition (1988: 35), but simple interpretations can have a powerful and helpful effect in the pastoral relationship.

The most accessible model that fosters interpretation is Malan's (1995) 'triangle of insight'. The corners of the triangle represent: past relationships, with associated events and feelings – 'back then'; present relationships, with associated events and feelings from the person's everyday life – 'out there'; and the current relationship in the room between the person and the helper – 'in here'. An interpretation links two or three of these aspects of the 'triangle of insight'. In the case of the school setting in the example above, the link was between 'out there' and 'in here'; at a later stage the same kind of interpretation could be used to make another link. 'When you talk about the way the school dominates your life and your lack of freedom, I wonder if it was like that with your parents when you were that age?' Interpretation requires experience and practice. Yet 'interpretation is not a substitute for careful listening and accurate reflection, and it does not shortcut the healing effects of time; but it fosters insight and self-knowledge' (Jacobs 1993a: 193).

4 Using challenge or confrontation in a way that enables progress

One caricature of counselling skills is where the helping person plays a passive role, nodding and agreeing with everything the client says. Another caricature is that counselling is a luxurious and unproductive form of indulgent navel-gazing. But like all caricatures, in which there is always an element of truth, these pictures fail to do justice to other elements, including that of challenge or confrontation. Both these terms suggest a gladiatorial image, but we might reframe this as the skill of offering a different perspective, which encourages people to reassess where they are, who they are, and what they might do. Some Christians assume that such a review will lead people to give up their faith and for that reason consider secular counselling to be dangerous (Collins 1988a: 11). If a person's faith is fragile it can benefit from being nurtured as well as challenged. Faith need not be an insubstantial, transitory illusion that melts under the slightest examination. A pastoral relationship helps precisely because it encourages a deeper exploration of personal narrative, dimly perceived emotions, troubling or perplexing thoughts, all of which may benefit from a different perspective being offered by the helper.

Culley lists the strategies for challenging as: confrontation; giving feedback; giving information; giving directives; counsellor self-disclosure; and immediacy (1991: 6). From a pastoral perspective I am less than happy with this list, especially the elements of confrontation or giving of directives. This is because some forms of Christian counselling are very confrontational, in that clients are perceived as needing to be faced with their sin, even where this is done in a thoughtful, caring, person-centred way. But the real challenge in counselling is to be faced with the strategies we use for defending ourselves, or the 'smoke screen' we put up to avoid facing ourselves. The person who always quotes the Bible and avoids expressing pain at his divorce needs a challenge that confronts his defences of splitting and rationalization. Similarly the giving of information or directives can too easily fall into the trap of pastoral care providing proof texts (key biblical texts used to support an action); or may evoke a familiar power dynamic where the pastoral carer is imbued with excessive authority.

The role of self-disclosure in Culley's list is one over which counselling theories are divided. I have known of people receiving pastoral care during a time of ill health, when hospital visiting times somehow gave their visitors unspoken permission to tell the patient all about their own illnesses. Since, as I have stressed throughout, the person who is being listened to is more important than the person who is doing the listening, self-disclosure can change that balance in an unhelpful way.

These more advanced skills already suggest that what is important is *how* they are used, not that they are indiscriminate tools that are wielded without thought or empathic feeling. If pastoral helpers reveal anything about themselves, it is most obviously going to be through the manner in which they use these skills, since they draw upon personal qualities, as much as the 'techniques' they use. The relational dimension of pastoral care and the personal qualities that are so vital in this inter-mediate stage of the helping process are the subject of the next chapter.

Chapter 8

Moving on – the intermediate stage of pastoral skills

Relational qualities

The importance of the quality of the relationship between the helper and the person in need has been introduced in earlier chapters. This relationship is crucial to all pastoral work, and, no matter how good one's technical skills and knowledge are, if they cannot be expressed in relationship this severely blunts their therapeutic impact. Yet this relationship is always a two-way process and, just as we are seeking to help and change another, that person in turn can help and change us. One of the key relational qualities required is to be open to the person we are helping at some deep level without using him or her to meet our own needs. Carl Jung put it this way. 'The doctor is effective only when he is afflicted. "Only the wounded physician heals." But when the doctor wears his personality like a coat of armour, he has no effect' (1995: 156). The garnering of religious, theological and psychological theories as well as pastoral experience and counselling skills is still no substitute for the real encounter that takes place between two people. This is a unique situation that draws on our history of every other relationship from our earliest times, memories that we carry within like some emotional hallmark. Orbach writes,

> As creatures of memory, of learning and development, the inevitable presence of emotional responses and expectations from past relationships is both instructive and unfortunate.

It allows us to anticipate the way things might go. It guides us as to when to relax and trust, and when to be wary. But at the same time it can prevent us from seeing who the other person is, what is possible in a situation, how we might be transformed and changed by it, or how we might ourselves have an impact on it.

(1999: 65–6)

It is in this context that I introduce three further relational qualities.

1 Staying with the person, especially when they get 'stuck'

As a child I remember being dressed in my best Sunday clothes for the visit of a grandmother. My twin sister and I wanted to go to the end of the road to wait for her arrival but decided to take a short cut across the back garden. What neither of us noticed until it was too late was that the garden had been rotavated and all that remained was churned-up earth, which after two days of rain had turned into a quagmire. We both sank up to our little knees in this mud and were to be seen holding hands and wailing for help. We survived being stuck by staying together. Yet feeling stuck in a pastoral relationship is trickier than the illustration perhaps suggests. It feels as if we are 'wading through treacle', as one person recently described a particular piece of pastoral work. Another common image or phrase is that of 'banging my head against a brick wall'. Such phrases appear to mean that pastor and client feel stuck, perhaps partly because the person may well be resistant for reasons like those outlined in Chapter 6.

Helpers experience three particular temptations when they find themselves in this position. The first is to blame themselves. It is very easy to feel that we are at fault. 'If only I was a trained counsellor', some ponder. The second temptation is to blame the client. 'If only they were not so resistant', others think. The third temptation is to assume an omnipotent role in order to help them cope with their anxiety. Like Jung's metaphor of the white-coated doctor donning a suit of armour, 'It is a chastening experience to see ourselves ... as a peeping tom, an autocrat, a prosecuting counsel, an oracle, or a saviour who washes the disciples' feet' (Hobson 1985: 180). Each of these reactions robs the helper of the value of staying with what is, by hankering after what might be. Part of caring is to know ourselves, including the way we often try to rescue ourselves or others when we become stuck or feel uncomfortable. It is chastening to realize that we may avoid others' pain by, for example, asking for more and more details. It is easy to become overly directive, or deal with 'stuckness' as if it were some intellectual battle that has to be won. The problem with being an oracle is that we may run out of wise things to say, and the trouble with being a saviour is that we are crucified in the end. The helper must hold back the powerful desire to rescue others, by allowing them to recognize where they are, even if that place means feeling stuck. In the past they may have had someone, often a parental figure, on hand to rescue them. When we reach adulthood, saviours do not come so readily to the rescue. Instead the good pastor is willing to be there, staying with the frustration even when there are no immediate answers or relief.

2 Avoiding taking responsibility for the client

This ability follows on from helping people when they and we are stuck. We are again tempted to leap into action rather than stay with the pain and 'stuckness' of another person's situation.

> One reason that some clients are clients is that they see themselves as victims, adversely affected by other people, the immediate social settings of life, society in its larger organizations and institutions, cultural prescriptions, or even internal forces. They feel they are no longer in control of their lives or some dimension of life. Therefore they talk extensively about these experiences . . . For some clients, talking . . . is a way of avoiding responsibility.
>
> (Egan 1994: 69)

This does not mean that we are irresponsible helpers who do nothing. Rayner sees self-scrutinizing responsibility as 'the keystone of helping professions' (1986: 170) but also warns of the dangers of unconscious gratification of 'yearnings for omnipotence' (1986: 169). There is an intoxicating feeling about being the one to which others turn for help. It can lead to grandiosity, to an inflated sense of self-importance or even, in Christian circles, to a false modesty that on the surface looks like humility but covers much more narcissistic needs. By letting people take responsibility for themselves, helpers 'model' how people can grow in their psychological or spiritual development. Yalom, an existential psychotherapist, views responsibility as a central issue for the person being helped.

> Every therapist knows that the crucial first step in therapy is the patient's assumption of responsibility for his or her life predicament. As long as one believes that one's problems are caused by some force or agency outside oneself, there is no leverage in therapy . . . why should one change oneself? . . . Since patients tend to resist assuming responsibility, therapists must develop techniques to make the patient aware of how they themselves create their own problems. A powerful technique . . . is the here-and-now focus.
>
> (1989: 8)

We provide a space where people can be heard in an empathic way and where vital connections can be made, so that they can experience their own responsibility as 'deeply enjoyable' (Yalom 1989). On the other hand, if we hold people in a childlike, dependent developmental stage by taking responsibility from them, they become 'very dull, shrunken people unable to face a crisis' (Yalom 1989: 170). This is the very antithesis of good pastoral care and counselling.

A key way in which we can avoid the temptation to take responsibility for another is by starting to take responsibility for ourselves. In this way we are taking a personal responsibility that is modelled and communicated at an unconscious level. Larry Parker, a counsellor who works with people who are addicted, expresses this eloquently in a chapter entitled 'Healing the "wounded healer" ':

> Jung believed that only the wounded physician heals – meaning that people who are wounded are fated to have to

deal continually with their own inner life and unconscious, which may enable them to contribute to others' healing. My journey in life has involved learning when I was wounded and what the wounding meant. I wasted a lot of time in the futile hope that some external source would assist. Eventually I reached the inescapable conclusion that I would have to take personal responsibility for my own healing . . . I am no longer attached to my wounds and I do not live in the past. Yet, on a soul and cellular level there is an indelible imprint of pain, which can be heard like an echo. I am driven to respond to the suffering of others as soon as I reverberate to the echo of their wounds, which is why I regard myself as being an example of a 'wounded healer': the counsellor I have become is the product of my learning from life experiences, with the training I found as a significant catalyst.

(1998: 195ff.)

Larry Parker's experience echoes that of many pastoral carers, and partly explains their desire to help others.

3 Expressing non-possessive warmth

At first this term may seem strange. It comes from research in the 1960s by Truax and Carkhuff (1967), which identified what helps people change. They found three specific qualities drawn from counselling and psychotherapy of all theoretical backgrounds. Pastoral care, counselling and theology have developed out of all recognition since the 1960s, but these qualities still have an important part to play. These qualities are:

- genuineness – which I explained in Chapter 5 as 'being real';
- accurate empathy – also looked at in Chapter 5 as 'expressing acceptance and empathy'; and
- non-possessive warmth, also known as 'unconditional positive regard' (Mearns and Thorne 1988: 59ff.) or 'personal warmth' (Hunter 1990: 1314).

Goodliff examines these qualities and finds them expressed in theology.

This emphasis upon the relational quality of the counselling exchange is not surprising given Christianity's understanding of the human existence following the pattern of the divine life: we are made in the image of God, and he is Being-in-relationship, the triune God. The healing of human psychological woundedness will come from relationships of trust, responsibility and empathy: precisely the kind of relationship that pastoral counsellors aspire to.

(1998: 180)

Mearns and Thorne go on to list the ways in which warmth is expressed in counselling; and they show how this also develops trust. 'Too little warmth will slow the development of trust and the process of counselling. There will be some cases where too great a show of warmth, however genuinely felt by the counsellor, may be difficult' (1988: 69). Mearns and Thorne identify a danger often found in a pastoral context. Members of a faith community, by virtue of a set of beliefs about the value of each person and the call to accept all people, are expected to be warm and friendly. The truth is that they are not, and people have discovered to their cost that some who initially seem warm and friendly appear so only because they have their own agenda. This is not a therapeutic or theological expression of warmth. Experiencing the warmth of another, someone who takes the time and trouble to relate to us in our pain or distress, feels like a precious gift, one that makes a connection, or creates a point of contact. Such a gift should be at the heart of every faith community. Goodliff explores this as a metaphor for the ultimate expression of pastoral care (1998: 123ff.). Hobson touches on this, not using the actual word warmth, but attempting to get at the heart of psychotherapy:

The *true voice of feeling* is a guiding ideal . . . it is not a simple emotion but a complex ordering and reordering of the experience of growing forms, especially by means of moving metaphors. It calls for 'sincerity' – a faithful expression of personal feeling.

(1985: 93)

Hobson's words may be difficult to understand, but they feel right in terms of communicating this vital warmth that is a hallmark of a deep pastoral relationship. The provision of non-possessive warmth as an expression of this dimension of pastoral care and counselling is vital, although it is not easily described or taught. It touches on inner resources of the helper, perhaps as a 'wounded healer' (Campbell 1986: 37ff.), a vivid concept developed by Nouwen (1994) and Ford (1999). Becoming a 'wounded healer' is another book in its own right, though it is a central theme in my earlier book, *Evangelicals in Exile: Wrestling with Theology and the Unconscious* (Ross 1997).

The demands on a helper using counselling skills are challenging, as we have seen in the previous chapters. Yet experience shows that these skills are attainable, and useful in a faith community or a pastoral context. Bond makes the point that the use of counselling skills may be more difficult than counselling because of 'more demanding circumstances' and that 'using counselling skills can be more skilled than counselling' (1993: 29ff.).

The helping skills model I am describing includes three stages, and with this chapter I conclude description of the second or intermediate stage of pastoral work. The next three chapters focus on the disengagement required for the closing stage of this helping skills model.

Chapter 9

Letting go – the closing stage of pastoral skills

Tasks

I can still recall the words of a former Baptist minister assessing an early sermon of mine. He said 'It was like a boat coming into harbour and tying up. Just when you thought it was about to happen, the boat drifted out again.' These words have stayed with me over the years and remind me how difficult it can be to come to the end of something that has become important to you. The skills I have looked at thus far enable good quality, professional pastoral care and counselling to take place. In this third stage my focus is on endings, which can in some ways be more difficult when a good helping relationship has been established than when it has failed to provide any help and has terminated prematurely.

'You're leaving me, just like everyone else. It's always the same when I get close to people – they go away. It's like a gaping wound that never heals. I thought you were different.' These were June's words to Simon, a curate in an Anglican church who was moving to become vicar in another parish. He had imagined that this parishioner, with whom he had always had a good relationship and whom he had helped at a time of bereavement, would have been pleased for him. He was taken aback by the anger and pain expressed in the tone of her voice and found himself speechless. Simon was experiencing the complexities of a multi-faceted pastoral role. He had failed to understand that his new future required him to attend to the ending of an existing role.

Helping skills: a relational approach	*Letting go – the closing stage*
Tasks	1 Bringing to a close a piece of work 2 Being aware of repeat losses and their impact 3 Enabling the person to be more authentic or integrated 4 Changing boundaries 5 Resourcing new aspects of personal and emotional narrative
Skills	1 Being clear about endings and keeping these in focus 2 Understanding the emotional impact of loss 3 Establishing what the person has gained and now values in him or herself
Relational qualities	1 Letting go and bearing ambivalence and anger 2 Believing in self, others and being 'good enough'

The closing stage of the helping process means the end of a particular relationship and it can be fraught with difficulties. Loss is a very difficult issue for most people because it touches on so many personal areas.

> A group of students on a counselling course decided to go for a meal to mark the end of their two years together. Although everyone had agreed to attend, one person failed to turn up. It transpired that he found endings very difficult, and although he had agreed to the meal in order to keep everyone else happy, he decided simply not to attend. This caused varying levels of concern and anger amongst the rest of the group; it was a reminder that no ending is ever complete.

There are always untimely moments, incomplete conversations, unspoken thoughts and feelings, which touch on areas deep within us of love, hate, pain and hope – usually a combination of them all. Helping somebody in a pastoral context requires a purposeful way of working that acknowledges this. It therefore involves the type of tasks described in this chapter.

1 Bringing to a close a piece of work

Most people do not want to be viewed as a 'task to be completed'. But if a pastoral carer fails to recognize the importance of the ending of the particular focused task in which he or she has been using counselling skills, he or she may also fail in truly helping the other. All pastoral carers in a faith community (even volunteers) have large workloads. One such volunteer who was approached to become a paid pastoral carer in her church declined. Her reasons for doing so were twofold. First, she thought that the church was a 'lousy employer'; secondly, she felt she would 'lose her freedom to say "no"'. But this is just the point. The pastor needs to be able to say 'no', or 'that is enough', in order to manage the pastoral workload, which means working intensively with some people some of the time, and providing more general or focused care for a wide range of others.

The ebb and flow of care in pastoral work makes constant demands. A pastoral carer on a training course said he would have a 'nervous breakdown' if everyone on his pastoral list wanted to see him. But some helpers find it very difficult to 'let go' of the people for whom they are pastorally responsible; and this often involves the carer's own needs rather than the needs of those they serve.

A pastoral consultant who explored this situation identified this as a significant weakness in the life of a faith community. Precisely because a certain woman in this faith community was good at building relationships with new people, she was given the lion's share of such pastoral work. But the consultant came to realize that everything had to be done in this woman's way; furthermore, some people were unhealthily dependent on her. Those she helped should have become more integrated into the life of the community. As the consultant said, 'She is like a mother hen, clucking around her brood, failing to realize that they are not chicks any more.'

When we have worked with a person using the counselling skills described in this book, it is for their benefit and ours that the work comes to a clear end. This does not mean that the pastoral relationship itself has come to an end; it simply recognizes that at this point in using counselling skills there is a specific 'letting go'.

2 Being aware of repeat losses and their impact

This was precisely the point which Simon had failed to understand. His careful work during the process of bereavement was commendable. He had arrived within hours when June had rung him up with the news that Bill was in intensive care following a major heart attack. In the ensuing 24 hours Simon had been a constant support and had been with June when Bill suffered another and fatal heart attack in hospital. His presence at a time of despair touched June profoundly at the core of her being and the heart of her faith. He represented for her the love and care of God that she could not otherwise feel. In the following weeks Simon helped June through the devastating storms of thought, feeling, belief, doubt and despair. His regular visits enabled her to tell the story of Bill's life through her shock, disbelief, anger, and depression. She felt she could talk to him about her husband, even when her own daughters tried to 'shut her up', thinking she was being morbid. Slowly through ongoing visits, as Simon listened, June came to a tenuous acceptance of her loss. His move threw her into panic and the renewed pain of loss. He failed to appreciate this, hence his hurt and surprise.

This situation demonstrates the need for a particular counselling skill: the ability to relate the experience of the present to the experiences of the past. A new loss has the capacity to trigger an old loss.

3 Enabling the person to be more authentic or integrated

Authenticity may seem a strange concept within the pastoral context. In many respects it is an ideal to which pastoral carers aspire, part of a lifelong quest, something which people experience though they may be unable to describe it. The listening skills described in Chapter 2 lay good foundations upon which integration and authenticity can be built. People who are heard in their pain and doubt, their hopes and fears, their guilt and forgiveness, may begin to feel what it is like to be genuinely accepted by God. From a Christian perspective, there is a vital incarnational dimension to helping others. The pastoral carer 'becomes the companion along the route of recovery and represents the family of faith and God's tangible presence' (Butler 1999: 143). From a Jewish perspective, the focus is on enabling a person to engage with religious traditions and rituals in a living and authentic way, rather than as a habitual or social act.

A church colleague had to announce that a church member had committed suicide. He broke down in tears as he told the congregation. His tears were seen as a sign of compassion, not of weakness, and because he was open in this way with the congregation, he touched hearts in an authentic way. Pastoral carers also long to see this authenticity in others, embracing and facing problems, rather than avoiding them.

---

4 Changing boundaries

One of the rewards of being a pastoral carer is the privilege of being allowed involvement in the life of another. I have shown earlier how important boundaries are to this involvement. They continue to be important at the close of any pastoral work, whatever level of counselling skills have been used. The role of the carer involves a certain kind of intimacy that, when an ending takes place, is lost to both the carer and the person being helped. It is one of the costs of pastoral contacts of any depth. Another phase of that person's journey is beginning, in which the helper will resume a more general involvement.

> It will be necessary . . . to make a definite shift in the caring ministry relationship, to put closure on a ministry that has served its purpose . . . Saying goodbye is always difficult, but not doing so and simply fading out of a person's life causes much more pain and hurt and can unravel all the effective ministry that has taken place. Closure of a caring relationship is as important as anything you do.
>
> (Butler 1999: 143)

This underlines again the importance of dealing with loss. People who find the ending of a pastoral relationship painful often find ways of trying to continue it.

Joe, a hospital chaplain, was very supportive to Howard whilst he was on the ward. It turned out that Howard had been let down by every authority figure in his past and wanted to hold on to this caring relationship. When he came back to hospital for outpatient appointments he called in to see Joe. He began calling in even when he did not have appointments and Joe found himself feeling increasingly trapped. Yet Joe found it difficult to say to Howard that he did not want to see him. He felt that the relationship had ended when Howard left as a patient. He felt guilty about not wanting to see Howard, but at that stage in his professional development he had not realized that so powerful a need to hold on could be established so quickly.

Boundaries are vital therefore when a specific phase in a pastoral relationship comes to an end. One of the tensions of pastoral work is that there is usually the possibility of ongoing contact. It would have helped both of them if Joe had been clearer about his boundaries as chaplain, and dealt with the difficult ending when Howard was no longer a patient.

5 Resourcing new aspects of personal and emotional narrative

When we listen we give others the opportunity to tell us about themselves and the things that have happened to them. As we listen to those parts of their life history they choose to tell us, we may discern layers of content and feeling, and see connections or links – often to past events.

> Communication through telling stories is a basic human activity. The Bible and other religious texts consist of sets of stories that teach moral lessons. The values and sense of identity of social groups have always been transmitted from generation to generation through legends and myths. At an everyday level, we are surrounded by stories: gossip, news reports, novels, cinema, TV soaps.
>
> (McLeod 1997: 29)

But McLeod makes a distinction between a story and a narrative that has significance for the work of the pastoral carer.

> A well-constructed story has a degree of dramatic quality, and conveys suspense, feelings and something about the personality of both the teller of the story and the characters within it . . . A story is told to 'make a point'. A narrative, by contrast, is . . . a general process of creating an account of what has happened. A narrative may include several discrete stories, but also include commentaries on these stories, linking passages and explanations.
>
> (1998: 145–6)

The counselling skills we use in a pastoral context enable people to tell their narrative. In a specific counselling session this may be through three or four stories told over the hour. In a pastoral context these stories may be told over months or years; the value of remembering and being remembered is at the heart of faith. It is a central theme in many of the Psalms and the later Prophets when Jewish people in exile long for a return home. At the communion service there is a specific point at which the words used are 'Do this in remembrance of me.' As we help people weave their stories together, they may discover aspects of their narrative which are depressingly familiar or encouragingly new. The long-term pastoral context may add insights and greater depth to the recalling of stories, which may form the basis of appropriate counselling skills to facilitate new personal, emotional and spiritual narratives.

What telling one's story does is allow for a new level of connection at a relational level and at a faith level. At this closing stage of this model there is an end to one form of narrative, the relational, and a return to a faith narrative. People may be able to see new insights into their faith story as informed by their own narrative and the narrative of the pastoral relationship. Narrative theology (Stroup 1981) has developed in recent years, and provides dynamic and inclusive ways (as opposed to the dominant doctrinal and exclusive way) of understanding the faith (McGrath 1996). Part of the task of helping in a faith community is to hold together the personal narrative and the faith story in a manner that liberates and enlightens. Pastoral carers link the faith narrative with the real, flesh and blood human narratives they encounter in others. For example, 'There is indeed the possibility of Christian healing working at this level, as the personal narrative of the person seeking counselling is reworked in the context of the broader Christian narrative' (Watts *et al.* 2002: 188). The person's story is now taken up into the narrative of the faith community bringing healing, and enriches both the individual and the community.

The overall task to which these different aspects contribute is that of closure. Endings seem at first straightforward. But, as the next chapter shows, they often require the use of particular skills.

Chapter 10

Letting go – the closing stage of pastoral skills

Skills

At this point in pastoral work, different but complementary skills are required to facilitate the ending. The ability to let go is not confined to pastoral care and counselling; it is a crucial part of the task of parents, allowing their children to grow up. This is not always easy and there is a maternal part in all of us that desires to go on nurturing and protecting, as well as an authoritarian part of us which finds it difficult to let children assume their own authority and responsibility. These can be positive caring functions in the right place and at the right time. But being a parent of adolescents means learning a new set of skills! Similarly, at this stage of the pastoral relationship there are particular skills about being able to let others go.

1 Being clear about endings and keeping these in focus

Letting go is hard for most people, as the following examples demonstrate. Feelings associated with being temporarily lost are magnified dramatically when we experience long-term or permanent loss. Ann Long, having had a hysterectomy, wrote 'Loss is the x-factor. It is the most profound happening in human existence, difficult to touch, impossible to convey and too indescribably painful for words' (Long 1997: 13). Loss is intense however commonplace it is, and as pastoral carers we continually discover this phenomenon in ourselves and in others, especially at this stage of the pastoral relationship. Having acknowledged the power and pain of loss, if we can then see it in the context of our faith and relationships, we may begin to discover how we can renew or reinvest that part of our lives.

It is always important to be clear about the end of even a simple pastoral encounter. Openly saying things like 'we have half an hour, and then I have to go to my next engagement' helps to clarify what time is available, allowing the person to choose what to talk about. The establishing of a clear time frame, with a beginning and an end, helps everybody. It helps the pastoral carer to attend fully to the person for that allotted time. It also ensures that the carers do not become overwhelmed by the constant demands of others. This clarity of focus enables a boundary to be put around the relationship and allows issues of limits of availability to be acknowledged. The end of a pastoral relationship also allows issues of loss and endings to be faced.

2 Understanding the emotional impact of loss

Mary, a pastoral visitor, went to visit Mrs Jones, an elderly widow. The visitor had come because Mrs Jones had not been to any of her regular church activities. Mrs Jones began by saying she didn't want to bother anyone but that she had not been out recently. She became tearful and talked about Billy going away. Billy, it transpired, was her dog that she described as 'the love of my life and now it seems so empty'. At this stage of a not unusual pastoral conversation, a pastoral carer has important decisions to make. Should Mary just unravel what Mrs Jones misses? The list might be long and include: affection; companionship; the ability to walk the streets safely; a regular routine of meeting other dog walkers; a reason to go to the shops; and something outside herself to be concerned about. Should she explore the emotional dimension of this apparently simple loss? The emotions might include: loneliness and the fear of being alone; anxiety about the future; an unpleasant reminder of death's unwelcome presence; guilt about not having done more, such as taking Billy to the vet; anger (often unexpressed, especially in a religious context) at the unfairness of life; and the aching longing that is felt in the depths of one's being but which is so difficult to identify. Should she, if the circumstances are right, explore what this loss means and how it might be connected to previous losses, such as the death of Mrs Jones's partner and the lack of contact with her children?

There is no 'right' answer. The decision depends on the person, the circumstances and the pastor's intuitive reading of the situation. Some carers might see intuition in spiritual terms as 'the leading of the Holy Spirit'. Most experiences of loss are accompanied by the feeling that nobody quite understands, or even that nobody wants to understand or care, especially when we are not entirely sure of the extent of the loss ourselves. Pastoral carers also need to decide how they will end this contact. In this example, Mary might see this as a 'one-off' visit, in which case she can help by listening to Mrs Jones; but she also needs to make clear to her the limited nature of the contact. Otherwise the loss Mrs Jones might feel will be magnified when the warmth of this human contact is itself withdrawn.

One problem is that we may have a blinkered view of the idea of loss. We may think simply in terms of death, especially in a faith community context where there are particular rites and roles in relation to funerals and visiting the bereaved family. Bereavement in terms of death itself is of course an important part of a pastor's work. A survey of rabbis in Los Angles found that bereavement was the second highest issue raised by those seeking help from rabbis (both orthodox and reform). But there are many other situations in which loss is experienced, including the ending of pastoral care relationships.

Losses other than by death may be just as traumatic, if harder to identify. A group of people were asked to 'brainstorm' loss, and the list they produced was staggering, in that it touched every part of human existence. It included: employment; faith; sanity; culture; opportunities; aspirations; hope; virginity; miscarriage; independence; confidence; self-esteem; disability; home; purpose; libido; power; role; health; identity; country; family; dignity; reputation; menopause; possessions; skills; divorce; moving house; pets; hair; security; rape; trust; attention; popularity; memory; sight; control; liberty; immortality and omnipotence. The person we are supporting may have experienced a combination of many losses, and it is important to identify a place where we can begin giving names to the losses and helping the person to find his or her own words

As a result of the research of such people as Elisabeth Kubler-Ross (1970), Colin Murray-Parkes (1986) and William Worden (1991), we understand more of the turmoil of pain and bereavement and have come to understand that people go through certain stages, and therefore need to accomplish key grief tasks. We know that people, when bereaved, experience a number of distinct phases in a process that usually last roughly two years, assuming they do not get stuck at a particular stage. These stages are disbelief, shock, disorientation and non-acceptance, followed by anger, guilt, depression, despair, and sometimes wanting to join the person. Eventually most people reach a stage of gradually learning to live without the lost person or lost object, punctuated by times when the grief is as acute as ever. At each of these stages the particular feeling predominates, and influences the whole of life. These stages may also apply to some aspects of ending pastoral work.

Shock

'It can't be true'; 'You don't mean it': such words convey the sense of shock when people hear of someone's loss. But shock is also experienced when the pastor says 'It's time for me to go', or 'I think the time is coming when my regular visits are no longer so necessary for you.' The pastoral relationship can have a powerful effect on a person's life, sometimes positively and sometimes negatively, especially if the person becomes very dependent on the carer. The end of such a relationship will always be painful, initially, and so needs careful preparation.

Anger

When shock, and sometimes numbness, has worn off, the uncomfortable reality sets in. Anger is one response, sometimes wanting to blame others. 'Whose fault is it?' 'Why didn't the ambulance come more quickly?' Such questions expose the anger we feel, often expressed in accusation and blame. Families bicker and fight, passing the guilt around in a tragic game of 'pass the parcel'. We blame God and rage at his indifference or impotence. 'What kind of God can allow this?' For some this anger is quiet, unexpressed and turned in on the self in the form of depression – like an autumnal fog, obscuring our way forward or back. Lethargy, sadness and sorrow seep into the bones of our being and at times suicide seems the obvious answer – no matter how strong our faith or religious convictions may be. As the months drift by, we are like a marooned boat barely kept afloat.

Gill became very angry when Joan told the church she was leaving for another parish. Gill felt that she had a 'special' relationship with Joan having helped her a great deal during the time of her partner's illness. Gill wanted to share in Joan's good news but it left her feeling upset, angry and then guilty.

Despair

Gill then started to believe that she was both a terrible Christian and a horrible person. Her enormous anger became turned in on herself and she found that not only was she depressed but that her faith had become bleak and despairing. She blamed herself for trusting Joan so much but knew that a crisis point had been reached when she felt suicidal. Her GP prescribed Prozac and six sessions with a counsellor based at the surgery. This counsellor helped Gill to see that there could be a link between the loss of an idealized and dependent relationship with her friend and the residual effects of her marriage breakdown five years before.

It is easy to idealize a friendship or a helping relationship, so that when it comes to an end there are painful consequences. Other people in Gill's situation become childlike and regress, recalling childhood patterns of behaviour. Like a schoolchild clinging to his mother's skirt, refusing to go to school, there can be a psychological clinging that is experienced at the end of a caring relationship. Some other responses are more rational but no less demanding, where people give reasons why they are a special case so that what applies to others need not apply to them. A key task faced by any pastoral carer at an end of a relationship is to bear the disappointment. Nobody likes being disappointed or disappointing others, and this is a special difficulty for carers. Disappointment needs facing, as it is a vitally healthy part of the way human beings develop psychologically. By facing and coping with disappointment, the person can discover not only that they survive but that they can find new resources within themselves.

Resolution

Despite the presence of loss, especially in bereavement, the routine of life continues and over the months and years a new perspective emerges. A husband whose wife died in the first year of their marriage said two years on 'I don't need to think about Mary the way I did before.' He had changed, adjusted; although still conscious of his past and uncertain about future relationships, he saw life as looking forward rather than back. Resolution includes learning to live without the loved one, and reorientation towards the future. In the case of a close friend, relation or partner, when they die they need not be forgotten but can be carried within the psyche or internal world of the surviving friend, relation or partner.

As we have seen, there are many non-death bereavements and part of the role of the carer is to help a person through these stages and complete their grief tasks (Worden 1991: 10ff.). At the end of the pastoral relationship a similar internalization of the process can take place. The experience of a reliable, caring figure forms into a memory that can be recalled, which includes the disappointment at the end of the relationship, but which builds a foundation for other good interpersonal relationships.

When we listen to people in their bereavement it is important that we do not assume that they are making a stage-by-stage progress according to a schedule laid down by research. Bereavement may be a developmental process, but it develops uniquely for each person; it is a mosaic of thoughts, feelings and actions, which accounts for the vast range of ways in which people cope with different traumatic events. We need to understand and respect the distinct ways in which people from different cultures and ethnic groups deal with death, and which enable them, whether or not they have faith or religious belief, to cope.

3 Establishing what the person has gained and now values in him or herself

One feature of a good helping relationship is when clients can discover that they are the authors of their own stories. The profound experience of loss or the impact of cumulative losses often forces people to re-examine and re-evaluate their lives. A liberating, exciting aspect of this discovery is that people may become able to find a voice for themselves, instead of being merely a passive listener to others. As they are listened to, with their feelings and faith authenticated as a vital part of them, people can discover who they are. The society we live in

> is one where on many fronts it becomes progressively more difficult for individuals to develop a firm sense of their own identity and then to hold onto it in the face of multifarious forces which seem to require constant readjustment both literally and psychologically.
>
> (Mearns and Thorne 2000: 14)

I have emphasized throughout that a key pastoral skill is to enable people to tell their story; at the ending something important will have been achieved when people can reauthor their own stories and discover unexpected layers, intriguing textures or new connections. From this fresh discovery of what it is to be a three-dimensional human being, body, mind and spirit, they can then begin, through the helping relationship, to discern their value and gain a new sense of being.

This focus on the value of being human is a message often lost within religious traditions that emphasize what people *cannot* do, rather than what they *can*. If this is reinforced by an upbringing that rewards certain behaviour and achievement, the task of reauthoring their stories becomes even more difficult. A tension may therefore arise where there is a clash between the person's story and his or her faith community. There is real skill in encouraging people to acknowledge their own story – and in giving them sufficient strength of belief in their own story to be able to face the wider faith community, which may not be as accepting of their story as the helper is.

There is an important role in reviewing what has been said, rehearsing it, rewording it or reframing it, perhaps, as the ending approaches. A different tension may emerge in some faith community contexts where there is a 'set text' and no other 'dialogue' is permitted. The concept of story and reauthoring is one means of enabling people to discover what they have gained from a helping relationship. Another way of doing this is to ask the person to engage in a review, where specific feedback is given by the client and the helper. A person being helped is able to end the process by identifying values, experiences or resources that he or she believes will contribute to his or her health. If the helper also gives feedback, it needs to be in terms of what the person has said, reinforcing what they have shared and learned; otherwise the temptation is to become like a doctor, who concludes the examination with a diagnosis and a prescription for the patient to take away.

There are then three crucial skills involved in endings: the first is being clear about them, speaking about them, referring to them at intervals, and keeping them in focus. The second is understanding the emotional impact and seeing the links in the ending to other losses that the person may have experienced. This can lead to an increased understanding about those earlier losses, as well as help in the loss of the pastoral relationship. It also involves recognizing a number of different feelings, which have been identified as stages of grief. The third skill is that of encouraging a review of what has been talked about, which may involve the rehearsal of a new story – or a new way of telling the person's story, in preparation for 'going it alone'. Ending is a time of re-evaluation and self-examination and is not always comfortable. It draws upon the personal resources of the helper as well, and it is the personal qualities involved in the closing stages of a pastoral relationship to which I now turn in concluding this model for the use of counselling skills.

Chapter 11

Letting go – the closing stage of pastoral skills

Relational qualities

Not only does the relationship between pastor and client in the end determine the outcome of the good use of skills and understanding of the tasks; it also models how to make a positive ending, through the way in which the pastor handles the different feelings involved. The specific qualities required at this stage of the helping relationship include: being able to let go; bearing ambivalence and/or anger; belief in the person being helped; belief in oneself; and acceptance that one is 'good enough'.

1 Letting go and bearing ambivalence and anger

In Chapter 9 I stressed the importance of the task of bringing a pastoral relationship to a close. This is done in the awareness that the pastoral context is one in which the meeting of pastor and client is likely to continue, albeit in different circumstances, such as being members of the same congregation. Despite this, for the moment, and at this time, there is a real ending. There will be mixed feelings. If we have been able to use counselling skills well enough in the pastoral relationship, and have pursued the relevant issues, the person being helped will have been touched in a unique way, and enriched by a sensitive and insightful pastoral relationship, in which that person's story has been heard and valued alongside his or her faith story. It is all the more painful when this comes to an end. The paradox is that the more impact a relationship has had upon a person the greater may well be his or her ambivalence, which may include some anger at the end of that relationship. The ending hooks into the powerful foundations laid down by early relationships including emotional memories that lie dormant like a sleeping tiger. 'In the earliest stages the human infant's attitude to his mother is that she must be there when she is needed, and there is hell to pay if she isn't' (Malan 1995: 191). A person can feel that in ending we have abandoned them; and this may link with an early memory that wakes the tiger.

People often find it very difficult to be angry in the church or with the clergy, at least to their face – so they experience mixed feelings that they find difficult to own. There may occasionally be over-reactions, and these are explicable in terms of early and painful memories of abandonment. Yet because these experiences occurred at a pre-verbal age, the person often has no conscious memory of them and cannot put words to these overwhelming feelings. The good pastoral carer has met deep needs in another that can leave the person feeling robbed, upset, angry and wanting to punish the person who has helped. Other patterns of reaction are covered by the range of attachments (identified in attachment theory) that helps explain the complex ambivalence that surrounds the end, albeit temporarily, of a good relationship (Holmes 1993). The difficult task of the pastoral carer may therefore be to allow and to bear the anger, if it is capable of being expressed; and to avoid retaliating out of one's own sense of hurt – after all, we have given much: why should this person be angry with us? What more do they want? When we are under pressure we need the self-awareness or insight that I describe later in this chapter.

Susie slammed the door as she left the room, shouting 'It was too much to expect you to understand.' She had been coming to see Carl for several weeks. During this time a good working alliance had been established, and Susie had talked about the way men had let her down in the past, and how she had just 'taken it'. Her sense of her own value had been affirmed through the very qualities of acceptance, warmth and trust in her pastor. Susie felt she really could trust Carl, and said 'What I like about you is that you don't interfere and you don't judge, even when I tell you really secret things.' Not surprisingly, she was angry when Carl reminded her that their helping relationship would come to an end after six weeks, as they had originally agreed. Carl was upset at the way the relationship ended and he talked it over with a mentor who helped to supervise his pastoral work. He began to see that Susie's dramatic and angry ending was natural and healthy, in that she had been able to be angry with a man; she felt a measure of equality in being able to react to Carl's reminder; and she knew she would not be punished in any way for her expression of feeling. Carl realized that endings are rarely smooth, and may feel abrupt, and that as the helper he had to bear a range of ambivalent and angry feelings.

Other clients feel relief at endings because, no matter how helpful the relationship has been, they fear becoming dependent. One advantage of the pastoral context is that dependency can be spread, inasmuch as the person who has received individual help may be able to receive support and affirmation from the wider community of faith. The community of faith provides continuity, and becomes a community of 'wounded healers' who can (in biblical terms) 'bear one another's burdens' by providing the loving acceptance that is at the heart of many faiths. Helping a person to let go of the relationship will come more easily where there has been an experience that has developed trust. This can form a secure base from which the person can explore aspects of previous relationships and attachment figures (Bowlby 1988: 138). Good though the relationships may have been, there are questions about whether the person has been allowed to grow up, encouraged to take responsibility for himself or herself and leave behind the pastoral relationship. The agony and anxiety of a type of psychological adolescence needs to be worked through; separating from authority and parental figures is an essential part of this. Again there can be a good deal of anger at being given responsibility for oneself, something that faith communities do not always encourage or find comfortable (Beit-Hallahmi and Argyle 1997: 176). Other aspects of anger in a religious context are helpfully discussed by Watts *et al.* (2002). One of the difficulties of pastoral work is that it can only deal with a limited focus. The demands on the pastor or pastoral carer make long-term counselling or intensive work impossible, even undesirable. In some sense it is in these longer term therapeutic relationships that such deep-seated issues of loss, abandonment and forms of attachment really belong. Yet the 'letting go' stage of any pastoral relationship needs careful attention to avoid repeating patterns from the past.

2 Believing in self, others and being 'good enough'

The child analyst Winnicott first used the term 'good enough' to suggest that a mother did not have to be the 'good' or the 'perfect' mother in order to help her child grow and develop, physically and psychologically (Jacobs 1995b; Gomez 1997). 'The best a real woman can do with an infant is to be sensitively good *enough* at the beginning' (Rodman 1987: 38). The best helpers with counselling skills can do is to be sensitively good enough not just at the beginning, but also at the end. This includes feeling good enough about themselves as well as about the person they are helping. This is not to say that helpers do not make mistakes. All helpers can learn to improve their practice and avoid making the same mistakes again, because pastoral work is never straightforward, and there will always be occasions when we mis-understand, fail to hear, or give a wrong or inadequate response. None of this is disastrous, especially when the relationship is 'good enough'. But many helpers display a tendency to devalue the work they do, and focus on failings more than on success.

Some people hear the term 'good enough' and think 'I need to be perfect' or 'I'm not good enough.' There is a danger in trying to tie up all the loose ends in an idealized quest for perfection. Endings are never neat and tidy. I recall handing in a 60,000 word dissertation that I had checked and rechecked and, as the volume left my hand, I spotted a mistake. It was too late and I had to let it go, hoping that it would be 'good enough'. At the end of a pastoral relationship it is impossible to have covered everything, healed everything, or been the perfect pastor, carer or counsellor. One indication of a good end point is that there has been a good enough relationship with a good enough change, even though probably much remains to be done. Pastoral care is neither first aid, nor is it long-term psychotherapy; it is somewhere in between. It is about creating an ongoing process, where the ending is handled in such a way as to encourage the person to carry the memory of the relationship within themselves. At times I have met people for whom I was formerly a pastor or counsellor. What often gets recalled are the very difficult experiences and the way in which particular issues and feelings were confronted rather than avoided, including the letting go at the end of the relationship (Ross 1997: 82ff.). Yet it is not always like that and people can still feel ambivalent about issues from the past; there the ending was not so helpful. One person recalled a comment I made fifteen years before that they had not really dealt with, even though they assured me at the time that they had forgiven me. Life, and pastoral life especially, has tangled and incomplete endings, which is all the more reason why they need specific attention.

Reviewing relational qualities

I indicated in Chapter 10 that a review at the end of a pastoral relationship can be helpful for the person, as well as the helper. It may therefore be a good point at which to review the qualities that enhance pastoral care and counselling; and to introduce in the next section the principle of reviewing or reflecting upon one's pastoral work.

I have already indicated that research into counselling outcomes has demonstrated that the key factor is the relationship. The theoretical orientation – psychodynamic, person-centred or narrative – is not important. Lazarus summarizes the qualities found in 'highly successful therapists' (which are also found in highly skilled helpers), many of which I have described in previous chapters. His list includes: a genuine respect for people; flexibility; a non-judgemental attitude; a good sense of humour; warmth; authenticity; and the willingness to recognize and reveal shortcomings.

The client too enables the helper in his or her task, contributing through 'motivation, cooperation, interest, concerns and expectations' (Corey 1996: 436). BACP looks at the same issue from a very different perspective, exploring the ethical demands of counselling. The Association states that the practitioner's personal qualities are 'of the utmost importance' to clients. Such qualities cannot be demanded; they develop out of the helper's own personhood. Such qualities are no less needed in a pastoral contact. The list that helpers 'are strongly encouraged to aspire to' include:

- empathy;
- sincerity;
- integrity;
- resilience;
- respect;
- humility;
- competence;
- fairness;
- wisdom;
- courage.

Many of these values are enshrined as virtues within religious traditions, so it is not surprising that they are a vital part of the relational qualities inherent in the pastoral support of others. The fact that they are not always achieved should not discourage anyone from believing they are attainable and hoping that they can be realized.

This raises a significant question: how do we assess these qualities within ourselves? The answer lies in self-awareness: awareness of what we think, feel and experience; of what we can remember; of how we react; of our strengths and weaknesses; and of our hurts and wounds. All these are aspects that combine to make us who we are. Self-awareness therefore is an essential quality in a helping person (Clarkson 1995: 279).

Stevens talks about three zones of awareness:

1 Awareness of the outside world. This is the actual sensory contact with objects and events in the present: what I now actually see, hear, smell, taste, or touch.
2 Awareness of the inside world. This is actual sensory contact with the inner events in the present: what I now actually feel from inside my skin – itches, muscular tensions and movements, physical manifestations of feelings and emotions, discomfort, well-being etc.
3 Awareness of fantasy activity. This includes all mental activity beyond present awareness of ongoing experience:

all explaining, imagining, interpreting, guessing, thinking, comparing, planning, remembering the past, anticipating the future, etc.

(1971: 5–6)

Stevens reminds us that if our awareness is limited in one of these three key areas, it will restrict awareness as a whole. New discoveries in any one area act as a catalyst for fresh awareness of other areas. Gerard Hughes, the noted author and spiritual director, describes awareness another way:

Our treasure lies in our inner life. It is our inner life which affects our perception of the world and determines our actions and reactions to it. We tend to ignore this inner life, but it refuses to be ignored . . . If ignored, the inner life will erupt . . . In religious language this inner life is called 'the soul', and the art of knowing it, healing it and harmonizing its forces is called spirituality. Religion should encourage us to become more aware of this inner life and should teach us to befriend it, for it is the source of our strength and storehouse of our wisdom.

(Hughes 1996: 8–9)

So how do we discover this treasure which lies within, yet often remains tantalizingly inaccessible? There are several possible routes; they include: personal experience of spiritual direction; or of counselling or psychotherapy, either individually or as part of a group; or spiritual and theological reflection, a model of which is described below.

A model of spiritual and theological reflection

This has five stages:

Making space

The ability to stand back or move away from all that is going on around is crucial for all those in a pastoral care role. Many, however, have become addicted to the 'buzz' of action, of being wanted, of being thought of as caring because they are always available. These addictions are connected with satisfying inner needs, rather than as evidence of pastoral effectiveness. Making space often means making time away from the demands of home, office or church. Moving to a special place for theological reflection removes the familiar reminders of demanding needs. Finding a place where we can relax and let our emotions catch up with us is important.

People do this in different ways. I used to travel to Oxford every month to see an academic supervisor, and I greatly looked forward to those days. Travelling on the coach allowed the demands to recede; walking to the college and across the park gave me feelings of freedom and space. It was at these times I rediscovered my 'self'. I learned to listen to what I was actually feeling, which the demands of ministerial life had repressed. It was often during these days that my awareness of God and my ability to listen to Him were repaired. Allowing time and space for a physical separation from our tasks, allowing emotional feedback and spiritual renewal, is a vital starting point in our theological reflection.

Clarifying issues

One way to stem the tide of overwhelming stressful demands is to begin identifying what the crucial issues are at that moment. The way of identifying such issues varies, partly according to temperament: a person with a more inward-looking nature may prefer to reflect, to be still and to use written words as means of clarifying issues; another with a more outward-looking nature may enjoy a more active approach such as discussion and interaction with others; theological reflection may take place in a group gathered for such a purpose or over a meal with a friend.

Expanding thinking

Making space and clarifying issues are preparation for the process of theological reflection. Reading a book from other disciplines, counselling, psychotherapy or fiction, for example, acts as a counterpoint to theology, and in turn illuminates and reflects on theology. This is an aspect of general revelation that is part of Christian theology – God being made known through the secular word, as it is claimed that all truth is God's truth. General revelation is where God is known through the thinking and feelings of all people, in nature, in mystical or spiritual experiences and other religions, including the worlds of counselling and psychotherapy. By reflecting on and thinking about what it is to be human we can gain new insights, as Rowan Williams puts it: 'All good stories change us if we hear them attentively; the most serious stories change us radically' (quoted in Migliore 1991: 34). This dynamic interplay of different disciplines can enable a reflection about theology and spirituality that leads to a new valuing of what God is doing in us, through us and, at times, despite us.

This is a two-way process. There is a vital role for theology to play in developing and expanding pastoral work, especially pastoral care and counselling. A good example is Goodliff's (1998) exploration of pastoral care in a postmodern context. 'Academic theology is now pursued to inform and illuminate practice, the past being plundered and sometimes (it would need to be confessed) re-invented to serve the needs of the present' (Wright 2002: 8).

Exploring feelings

Spiritual or theological reflection ignores feelings at its peril. Christian faith is an incarnate, embodied, experiential faith that needs to accept the place of feelings as much as the place of ideas. Other faith communities value feelings in a vital way as part of their tradition. The protective defences referred to in Chapter 6 allow little place for feelings. Yet we need both space and safe boundaries (a holy place, a quiet room, a secure relationship) in order to rediscover the emotional wellspring of our being and allow lost feelings, submerged feelings, suppressed feelings to emerge from darkness to light. Since pastoral work puts us in touch with a whole range of emotional situations, reflection upon them is especially important.

Determining action

Once we have been through this process of reflection and discovery, there comes the time to plan what comes next. We may
discover how much we have allowed ourselves to be taken over
and manipulated by the needs of others. Action may need to be
checked out with others whom we trust, because we are not
always realistic about what we can do.

Personal experience of spiritual direction and/or counselling or psychotherapy

Self-awareness rarely happens on its own, and certainly not in a
vacuum. It is not a solitary exercise, but is facilitated through
encounters with others, who can sharpen our thoughts and help
uncover our feelings. Through the agency of another we can
become much more aware of the deeper self. Perhaps it is this that
is the key factor that keeps people coming back to counselling or
psychotherapy. Although some clients may be seeking to 'get
something fixed', more often they want to grow, with the help
of another who offers opportunities for a special insight into their
lives. Another such person who offers a unique insight is a
spiritual director:

> Most if not all religions have within their framework a place,
> sometimes centrally, sometimes peripherally, for a 'spiritual
> guide', a man or woman who is seen to be the repository of a
> special wisdom that is in touch with the divine: the Hindu
> 'guru'; the Buddhist 'master'; the 'shaman' of northern Asia
> and native American traditional religion; and the 'rebbe' of
> Hasidic Judaism . . . In the Christian tradition: he or she is
> desert-dweller, soul-friend and midwife . . . In each of these
> three priestly metaphors, the spirituality is a spirituality of
> presence.
>
> (Hurding 1998: 287)

I have emphasized already that it is vital that helpers avoid
meeting their own needs through helping others. Watts addresses
this issue in relation to clergy, although what he writes applies

equally to all those who are in positions of power within religious institutions:

> Like many people in the caring professions, clergy may be meeting their own emotional needs by helping other people. They can project their own neediness onto members of the congregation, and meet their needs vicariously while ostensibly helping other people. This can result in an unfortunate pattern of encouraging excessive dependency in the congregation to maintain the minister's own emotional adjustment. Finally, in most people there is both a nice 'persona' (i.e. mask) and a darker 'shadow' side. People in caring professions . . . may be over identified with the nice side and try to ignore the darker side of their personality. This becomes difficult to maintain, and people can crack under the strain of trying to do so. Equally, the unacknowledged dark side of the personality can be projected onto those being cared for, leading to an unreasonable resentment of them. Once again the important thing is for ministers to be as clearly conscious as possible of what may be going on in their caring relationships.
>
> (Watts *et al.* 2002: 263)

But we of course do have our own needs, and it is appropriate that these should be met as well – not in helping others, but in finding opportunities to reflect upon those needs, and address them, in spiritual direction, in personal counselling, and in self-reflection. Caring for oneself is a vital aspect of being in a caring profession.

This encouragement of personal reflection also helps in pastoral work, because it can reveal the 'blind spots' within us. And of course, returning to the main theme of these last three chapters, it helps in managing the complex feelings that are experienced in 'letting go', especially of a relationship which has been valuable. If we have our own resources, we do not need to hold on to those we help, but can let them go their own way.

At this point I reach the end of the last part of the model I introduced in Chapter 9. The three stages of the helping relationship have each been considered under three headings: tasks, skills and relational qualities. This integrative model has brought together key features from person-centred counselling that focuses on the quality of the relationship between two people, one of whom is in a helping role. I have drawn upon such writers as Thorne (1998) and Oden (1978) from a Christian background; and Katz (1985) from a Jewish background, all of whom see important parallels between the offering of empathy, unconditional positive regard and congruence and how a person living out the best qualities enshrined in their faith tradition will respond to another in need. Linked to this I have shown the importance of unconscious processes, working with the past in the present and in the transference relationship, and styles of attachment. These are found in psychodynamic theory and counselling (Malan 1995; Jacobs 1988, 1993a, 1998), and object relations and attachment theory (Bowlby 1988; Holmes 1993; Gomez 1997). I have drawn upon other therapeutic work that is based on psychodynamic theory and insights but expressed in relational terms, such as in Hobson (1985), Lomas (1993, 1999), Coltart (1993, 1996) and Orbach (1999).

These different theoretical perspectives have been enlisted to map ways of helping people to develop links between their life story, with all its emotions; their unconscious story as it may emerge in the pastoral relationship; and their here and now story, which in turn may be embedded in, or can be integrated with, their faith story. The emphasis on narrative and the holding together of stories that sometimes conflict, and at other times serve as a catalyst to one another, is a distinctive contribution of this book, which finds echoes in the work of McLeod (1997) and Lyall (2001).

The danger of such an integrative model is that its very inclusiveness can appear daunting. There is so much to think about and contain! Added to this it is a fact that often faith communities have not been models of best practice in human relations. It is here where 'supervision' or 'mentoring' can be of such value, since it is in the discussion of the practice of pastoral work itself that the learning becomes integrated. Yet it is in the very practice of pastoral work, using counselling skills, as many of the examples in these chapters have shown, that the real rewards lie. When people grow and develop, and discover through insight and a trusting relationship lessons about themselves that help them to integrate their experience, it is a pleasure to have played a part in that process. But more than this, some of those people will make their own contribution not just to the pastors or carers who have helped them, but to the health of the whole faith community as well. This model then can help equip them, arising out of their own experience of being helped, to find new areas of growth and service in their relationships with others.

The final chapters apply this relational helping model to some of the wider issues and concerns experienced by faith communities.

Part Two

Key issues in the pastoral context

Chapter 12

Conflicts with beliefs and values

Liz, my twin sister, stared at me with dark brown eyes and said 'You dare.' What an incredible and irresistible challenge for a twin brother to rise to! Inevitably I did and a fight ensued. I can look back to our childhood with warmth and affection whilst recognizing that there was a great deal of conflict, both between us as daggers-drawn enemies, and as allies against our other siblings. It seems that conflict is an intrinsic part of what it is to be human.

The Genesis account of Adam and Eve points this out clearly. As theological students we were engaged in debate with a visiting lecturer, a rabbi from Jews College (as it was then known) in London. When asked about his understanding of Genesis, he talked about its metaphorical and figurative qualities, at which point several students very aggressively responded concerning the historicity of this account. This led to other verbal attacks in which the rabbi was given little opportunity to respond. It was an uncomfortable and I dare say an unchristian experience of conflict. Two faith communities with a history of hostility and conflict could not even engage in simple debate.

There are times when our sense of faith is so insecure that the only response is to attack. Faith communities, like every other community, find conflict difficult to handle, although the presence of a conflict is not wrong in itself. One of the fundamental ways we grow as people is to test our thinking and behaviour out on others; by the messages we receive back from them we add to our sense of self. Conflict only happens over things we are passionate about and it can make us examine what is real and what we need to change.

Inevitably faith beliefs and values clash with what we personally want or need. A degree of conformity can be a sterile and disabling aspect of personality, as Jesus so clearly pointed out through the character of the elder brother in the story of the prodigal son (Luke 15), a subject upon which Nouwen (1992) provides a valuable series of reflections.

Carol felt just as abandoned as the prodigal son of the biblical story. She had fallen in love with Greg, a colleague at work. At the age of 24 Carol felt she was 'on the shelf', and this was not helped by the fact that many of her contemporaries had been to university and had come back with not only a degree but also a partner. Greg became the source of all hope for her, yet this raised a huge problem for her, because as part of an evangelical church Carol had always been taught, 'Do not be yoked together with unbelievers' (II Corinthians 6:14), especially in opposite-sex relationships.

This is not just an issue that Christians face. Intermarriage has become a major concern for Judaism as marrying outside the faith is, in effect, to leave it. Jonathan Sacks, the Chief Rabbi of the United Hebrew Congregations, was asked how he would cope if his son came home and asked to marry outside the faith. Such possibilities crystallize the key issues of faith and emotion, sometimes involving personal choice over religious conviction.

These issues raise questions of how we deal with such conflicts about faith and values in the pastoral process. Do we begin with affirming the faith position as a way of offering the care that a faith community has built up over centuries? A Christian carer might begin by exploring the tensions that mixed faith relationships could result in, as well as sharing the experience that many in similar situations have found: that they almost extinguish faith and sometimes reduce it to the level of a flickering candle in a draughty room. They give rise to split loyalties and one or other partner often finds it difficult to play a meaningful and active role in the life of a faith community. Jonathan Sacks's response was similar. He would try to discourage his son, hoping that Judaism and its continuity would mean enough to him to persuade him to want to create a Jewish family and raise Jewish children (1995: 118). Here personal choice is influenced by religious belief. Many Christians and many Jews choose not to marry outside the faith, and the role of church and faith community workers may be seen as trying to prevent this from happening.

Other pastoral carers might begin where Carol is, and with her need to be loved, her sense of completeness in finding another with whom she wants to share her life, her search for a partner and a mate to fulfil a desire to be a mother. Certainly Carol's situation makes us ask searching questions of ourselves. Where are we in the process of bridging faith and action, belief and behaviour? Such a conflict makes searching demands on us as carers, and forces us to examine assumptions about the way we work. Unless we discover these assumptions for ourselves we will be less clear about what kind of care we offer to others.

This is especially true in the area of religious beliefs and values. One of the religious values held by church or faith communities is the expectation that we care for all people in all situations. So what do we do when someone comes to us with a personal issue that conflicts with faith? The answer is both simple and complex. Starting from where we are, we bridge the two aspects of faith and humanness. The result can be a more genuine commitment to a belief or a moral value, because we encounter it through experience and therefore no longer regard it at some abstract level of understanding. We also discover more about ourselves, because having to engage with another person touches what we are feeling. Part of growing up includes not always getting what we want. Willingness to say 'no' to some things increases the value of our 'yes' choices, made in the context of a faith community that undergirds the choices we make. The pastoral carer's role sometimes includes wrestling with the pain and agony of difficult choices, balancing conflicting demands, valuing risk, and not being dependent upon divine or faith community approval.

But I have already made a huge assumption about Carol, when I assume I can give any help at all. What is vital to find out first is what Carol really feels about the problem, and whether or not she wants to do anything with it. What are *her* assumptions or expectations? There is no way I can know unless I ask Carol. It is vital, therefore, when we go into pastoral situations, that we not only recognize our own assumptions, but also that we check out the assumptions of the person we seek to help. As well as asking what our assumptions are, we can also question what kind of role the pastor plays and what motivation lies behind the role. This might include being:

- an expert with specialist advice to offer;
- a guide along a journey;
- a fellow traveller also on a journey, part of which is to be shared;
- a fellow victim, looking for someone to listen as much as wanting to listen to another;
- a person of faith wanting to help others, for motives that spring from that faith;
- someone in search of another that will make them more complete;
- one who tries to prove to God how good they are (even if we do not feel it) by all the helpful things we do for others;
- a compulsive rescuer that can care for anyone and everyone;
- someone who takes on more and more, but duty prevents them from saying 'no'.

If we begin to understand ourselves we may get a better sense of what we are trying to achieve in being a pastor to others. In the light of that I suggest one way of approaching Carol's dilemma.

The first thing a pastor might do (something that is often done unconsciously and not always recognized) is to remember what he or she knows and feels about Carol. In this case the pastor knew that she was clever, but not exceptionally so, and she worked very hard in her job. She had been part of a crowd of young people where she expressed her own brand of humour and she seemed to like being the centre of attention. Her father was brusque and dominating, and her mother quiet and acquiescent. In fact the pastor knew a great deal about Carol, which she had not realized until she deliberately sat down to think about the situation. Often pastoral care is exercised on the basis of more knowledge and understanding than we realize, yet it is important to bring into focus all the aspects in order to enhance the task of caring.

Yet relationship involves not just what we know; it includes what we feel. Knowing what is happening in our feelings is a vital factor since they gives us clues about the person and suggest ways in which we can establish relationship with the other person. The pastor also felt Carol was rather fragile and would go along with things for a 'quiet life'; that there was a rather compliant surface, beneath which a rather more interesting person could be found. Carol saw the pastor in the pastor's home. How and where pastoral care takes place is an important but often neglected aspect of the helping relationship. A great deal of attention is given in counselling literature about this and it is an area from which helping relationships using counselling skills can learn. Issues of power (which I explore later) and safety need consideration. The pastor asked how she was feeling and Carol replied that she had been struggling spiritually, finding it difficult to pray or read the Bible.

What was she saying? Nothing. Or rather, what she thought the pastor would want to hear. Carol was waiting to discover if the pastor was willing to see beyond the obvious and so the pastor took this opportunity to delve a little further. She asked what it was like at work. This was a simple and direct question that allowed Carol to answer factually, without feeling she had to disclose anything unless she chose to. The pastor reflected back to Carol what she was herself feeling, saying 'It all seems rather grey and lonely to me as you describe it.' Carol was visibly moved and she sat back in the seat, her face relaxing and eyes opening wider. They talked about a few things related to work and home. Part of the discipline of a pastoral conversation is the ability to hold onto feelings and reactions in order to listen better to the other person; and only then to use them sparingly, as long as they advance the relationship. It felt as if Carol was beginning to say something significant when she talked about those she had met at work and how alone she had felt at church. Here she was facing the conflict with her faith tradition, both her own and her parents'. When Carol had finished talking she looked almost shocked and said 'I didn't mean to say all that.' At this point it was important that the pastor stepped with utmost caution, the ice feeling at that point very thin.

Carol had risked telling her story, having been drawn into a new layer of relationship through the quality of attentive listening. What Carol realized was that she had said what she really wanted to say, but was now vulnerable to criticism or judgement. Would it have helped Carol to remind her then of one interpretation of her faith tradition? I think not, even though the pastor sensed that Carol was waiting for some kind of authoritative judgement, given her role within the church community. It would have been so easy to add to the critical, parental and authoritative voices that seemed to drown out Carol's voice. She had risked saying things, perhaps for the very first time. She had risked expressing herself and being exposed to another. The pastor responded by saying that it is always difficult when thinking and feelings collide, that sometimes it leaves us feeling trapped and not sure what to do. Carol sighed and some tears formed in her eyes. The pastor also ventured that it sounded as if life was quite lonely, and that it feels really good when we have a special friend.

They had agreed at the start of their time together that there was about an hour for the session. Time boundaries are again a crucial aspect of the counselling relationship (McLoughlin 1995) but have received little attention in a pastoral context. Yet time boundaries are especially important in a pastoral context, precisely because they enable two people to have some sense of what they are working within. Although time pressures face all faith community workers, people are helped in the telling of their story by knowing the points that start and end the session (Boyd and Lynch 1999: 66). The time together was up and the pastor suggested that if she wanted they could talk again. Carol saw her again several weeks later and told her she had arranged to go out with a girlfriend from church. She was not sure what she was going to do, but talking made her realize that God could be trusted to work things out and that God trusted her in a way that she had not sensed before. The message that Carol had heard gave her a new, more positive sense of self that had always been present, albeit in embryonic form. She had been given space to tell her story, free from judgement, by having someone listen to what was present just below the surface. She had needed a little encouragement for the real issue to surface, namely her loneliness. She had been offered the opportunity to explore how she felt about the tension arising from her dilemma. She came to see that she had 'idealized' the person at work and her relationship with him. She was fully aware of the pitfalls of this form of relationship, but she might have held on to it if she had been told that she was doing the 'wrong' thing, since her need to rebel had echoes of her family context, and was part of the overall picture.

In some ways Carol's problem seems relatively easy to explore, but only perhaps because she found a resolution where there was in the end no conflict between faith and feelings. There are other situations that cause much greater conflict in carers because there is no easy answer. The situation cannot be resolved and they are therefore left with a bewildering variety of painful feelings and deep theological questions that God does not appear to answer. Caring for people can be profoundly upsetting and unsettling for carers, as well as enormously rewarding.

Tracey's experience is another example. As Frank sat in his study looking out of the window he saw Tracey, a church member, walking past the house backwards and forwards several times. This seemed rather odd and he went out into the street to invite her in, which he did in a friendly, cheery way. Any cheer went out of his soul when Tracey looked at him and he saw a swollen, distended, black and blue face. Frank felt shock, concern, compassion and anger in a swirling vortex of feeling. She came in and he made her a cup of tea. Tracey told Frank that Jim had beaten her up again, although this was the first time Frank had any knowledge of this. Tracey could not report Jim because he was a policeman and could lose his job as a result of this assault. He had a leading role in the church and was looked to as a role model for being a strong Christian in a difficult environment. 'He just gets wound up. It's my fault really – I shouldn't have provoked him. You won't tell him I've been here, will you? Promise me you won't', she pleaded. What could Frank do? Should he care for Tracey by helping her in the short term and agreeing with her? Or should he care for her in the longer term by addressing the violence that always carries the threat of disability and even death? How do you square the public image of Jim, who declares to all that God uses him in powerful ways in his work to help others, with the private figure who abuses his power to hurt physically and psychologically?

Pastoral carers often find these tensions in the faith community; they are invited into the private agony in which so many people live. What are the issues in this situation? There is a personal issue for Tracey who needs her story to be heard and believed and has taken the risk of speaking the truth; she is no longer pretending that she walked into a door. If anything Tracey has minimized the violence rather than dramatized it. There is a safety issue for Tracey and her children. They are teenagers and free from her husband's violent outbursts, though not immune from the effects of destructive psychological patterns. Not surprisingly they have little time for the church. There is a church issue of the private conduct of an individual destroying any value of their public contribution to faith and church. How is this to be addressed, especially since Jim is standing for a leadership role in the church that he is almost certain to be elected to? There is also a faith issue – how can Jim reconcile belief in a loving God; respect others, especially the vulnerable and powerless; and value their creation in God's image – all important beliefs – when he treats his wife this way? Jesus reserved his sternest words for religious hypocrites.

A helpful place to begin here is to determine the respective priorities of these competing and conflicting claims. What is the most caring thing for Tracey? Perhaps Frank should start by asking her what she wants. After the initial relief of telling him and being believed, Tracey may now be in a place where she can think more clearly. She has been given some temporary safety, although ongoing safety is vital if her thinking is to make further progress in this complex and painful situation. Any decision Tracey makes has an element of risk, which is added to by not feeling safe enough to contact statutory authorities such as social services or the police. The temptation is to make decisions for Tracey, which in some ways is just as dominating, as it keeps her in the position of being powerless. Domestic violence is about power, control, ownership and rights, so it is vital not to repeat these patterns, even for supposedly helpful and caring reasons. Any decisions need to be Tracey's, since she has to live with the consequences.

The urgency in this situation was to reassure Tracey that she would be safe. In situations like Tracey's women experiencing violence have not been believed; the faith community leader has even rung the husband telling him to come and collect his hysterical wife. It seemed to Frank that the priority was the person rather than the institution, although he recognized that what he had been told had implications for the faith community and could not be swept under the carpet. He helped her find a place of safety, where she could begin to see the wider issues and implications in a way that she was too traumatized to do up to that point. It would take Tracey time to come to a decision to leave her husband, a decision made more difficult because questions about divorce are still a burning issue in many faith communities. But if Tracey had chosen not to address the violence it would have left the faith community, and Frank, to whom she has spoken in confidence, with an ongoing issue, that could perhaps only be addressed from a different perspective of education and raising awareness.

When beliefs and values come into conflict with human needs pastoral carers often find themselves bridging the tension between the two. We all need to be aware of how we work and from which side of this tension we start out. Jonathan Magonet explores this matter in *Religious Tensions in Counselling*. He tells of an Orthodox rabbi and trained counsellor addressing a meeting of Jewish counsellors:

> The aggression directed at him was astonishing . . . when the same stereotyped thinking and prejudice and anger emerge from counsellors, it becomes more than a bit disturbing. The rabbi was challenged . . . Surely his authoritarian tradition could not leave him free to deal with the real problems that people present. After all the task of the minister of religion was to inculcate and enforce certain values and that of the counsellor was to be a neutral person who enabled the client to find their own particular way . . . His reply was disarming. Because he knew the religious values of his tradition and had come to terms with them in his own personal life he was able to build into his counselling a conscious awareness of the limits within which he was working . . . He was then able to point out that if the questioners had *not* examined in a mature adult way their own relationship to religious tradition then they ran the risk of bringing unresolved difficulties into the client/counsellor relationship.
>
> (1988: 145)

However, there are times when the two cannot be bridged, and then the pastor has to live with a different tension: that of failing to resolve an issue which still deeply affects both the pastor and the person he or she has tried to help. Such conflicts might, however, be a catalyst to a rediscovery that some people call post-traumatic growth (Linley and Joseph 2002).

Tracey's experience faces faith communities with another crucial issue. It is an issue that has assumed even greater import-ance in the current climate of social, cultural and philosophical change ushered in by postmodernism (Lyall 1999). How do institutions cope when the values/beliefs they enshrine conflict with people's needs? To take Tracey's situation one step further, she decided to divorce her abusive husband. She needed to be free from the abusive relationship. Her faith community's belief was that divorce was wrong – with adultery being the only exception, and even this was disputed. This clash between needs and values is always going to be a significant aspect of faith community life. The tension is between holding to ideals, that have been given authority and power by tradition and which have been ascribed to God's revelation, and meeting the need of a person. It is no less difficult when following through the tasks, skills and qualities of the helping relationship model described in this book. Yet the model illuminates the role taken on by those who care for and counsel others. What is important is that they contain rather than deny these dilemmas.

There are three possible routes to take in such situations: recognition of conflict as potential growth; willingness to give permission; and an understanding of the nature of power.

Conflict as potential growth

Conflict is a taboo subject in faith communities. A new minister coming into a church situation can see the damage from her pre-decessor and his conflictual relationship with the church but either nobody will talk about it, or a few nurse their grievances and are all too willing to vent their spleen. There is 'an ex-pectation that church should always be a perfect, conflict-free environment; everyone should be "nice"' (Watts *et al.* 2002: 232). Bland phrases such as 'It's all water under the bridge', or 'Don't muddy clean waters' are used to avoid the painful retelling of a previous conflict. Wounds are hidden and memories are forced underground, at the cost of lessons that can be learnt from the conflict. The idea that conflict can be a source of potential growth is treated with suspicion in many faith communities. It is easier to withdraw or hide. A client described what this meant for him:

> I can only deal with a limited amount of experience. This is especially so when the information is, or seems to be, contradictory when I am faced with *conflict*. I can continue to create my personal world only by some degree of exclusion, by restricting what I perceive, what I feel, and what I think. I cannot cope with everything.
>
> (Hobson 1985: 42)

Many of the insights about conflict come from psycho-analytic theory, which sees it as often unconscious, yet as a fundamental aspect of the human condition. Therapists either try to help clients become aware of it and therefore able to choose how to deal with it; or contain the conflict and detoxify until clients can handle it themselves; or through attention to clients make good a deficit and allow them to rebuild a secure sense of self (Bateman and Holmes 1995: 23).

Faith communities are faced with similar possibilities. Kornfeld (1998: 23ff.) identifies the positive and negative features that enable faith communities to deal with conflict.

What is immediately apparent is that pastoral carers, by the nature of their training and their involvement with people, find themselves predominantly in the left hand column, but they are working in a faith community that is predominantly represented in the right hand column. As a consequence the holding process they engage in, offering a relational model, places even greater burdens on them. At times it feels that the pastoral task is about surviving the conflict between these two sets of interest, and this can dim the vision of conflict as a potential for growth both for people and faith communities. Watts *et al.* (2002: 234) use a different framework for assessing conflict, although they still recognize its growth potential. Using a graph they locate the two axes as 'issue' (this could also mean belief or value) versus 'relationship'. There are five ways or coping styles for holding these two in tension: accommodation, collaboration, compromise, avoiding and competition. Those who most

Dealing with conflict: positive features	*Dealing with conflict: negative features*
A positive attitude	A negative attitude. Believe 'conflict' and 'fight' are the same
Have agreed to differ and resolved to love	Do not understand the role of conflict
Work to understand differences	Are frightened by difference. Value is placed on people being similar. Change is threatening
A process to be worked through, not as a problem in and of itself	See conflict as a problem. The potential for conflict needs to be eliminated wherever possible
Accept anger when it arises	Cannot accept anger and as it cannot be expressed, it becomes resentment expressed in covert, hidden ways
Are able to tolerate ambiguity. See less need for a rigid approach	Cannot accept ambiguity because there is only one acceptable way. The community is more comfortable with 'right' v. 'wrong'
Are intentional about learning to listen to each other and to God. Are able to affirm one another and have formal and informal ways of working through differences	Believe they are listening to each other, though often make assumptions based on the belief they are alike. Rely on religious leaders for the interpretation of God's will

emphasize issues, beliefs and values also favour avoiding and competition coping styles (equating to Kornfeld's negative features of dealing with conflict). Those that most emphasize relationship favour accommodation and collaboration as coping styles (equating to Kornfeld's positive features of dealing with conflict). The central balancing style identified by Watts, Nye and Savage is that of compromise:

> Some of us may have experienced the trauma of church conflicts escalating out of control. This deeply damaging

experience need not occur . . . conflict in church can be an opportunity to achieve great strides forward in the redemption of sin's imprint in our personality and relationships . . . Ideally the church should be a safe place for sin to be exposed and dealt with, and its attendant wounds to be bathed in compassion.

(2002: 237)

What is hard is that often it is pastoral helpers who have to bathe the wounds that have been inflicted by others within the faith community, by those who would rather not face the pain and issues raised by human needs, by vulnerability and by weakness.

Willingness to give permission

The second way of containing the tensions that arise from faith and values is to allow people being helped to acknowledge that they are human and take the risk of being real. Such permission is not necessarily stated openly, although people sometimes need a helping phrase to cry, or to express their anger. The permission I have in mind is also simply 'being with'. By being a fellow traveller on a shared journey the person being helped senses that it is all right to express feelings, or to utter the unthinkable. The pastoral relationship encourages people to tell their story, just as it is, without the usual pretence or the need to make it more palatable.

There appear to me to be five areas where providing such permission is most needed in faith communities. First, people want permission to ask important questions. One such question is 'Why?' in the face of suffering (Ross 1999: 40), when it is all too easy for those in the faith community to try and answer this by reference to standard beliefs and values. In doing so the emotional pain of the question is overlooked, and the psychological impact of experience coming into conflict with beliefs and values is often neglected. Second, people want permission to express doubt. In a faith community where beliefs and values are posited as certainties, the ability to make room for genuine doubt is often lacking. Doubt has different dimensions: theological (Tidball

1988), philosophical (Hookway 1995: 205), social and cultural (Pattison 2000: 142), psychological (Beck 1999) and pastoral (Thomas 1987; Pruyser 1990) – yet with a few exceptions (Jacobs 1993b) it is a subject missing in much pastoral and counselling literature. Doubt is, however, vitally present in some of the best devotional literature, such as that by Nouwen, who holds together theological and psychological insights (Ford 1999). The pastoral encounter is usually the only safe space for people to dare to be honest about their doubts, although to begin with they may feel prohibited from expressing them, not only because of the publicly stated beliefs and values of their faith community, but also by their assumption that doubt is what the minister would most frown upon. 'Personal religion is a constant encounter and engagement with doubt, and as one's awareness of limitation increases with knowledge so too does doubt. The more we know of God the stronger and more subtle the attack from doubt' (Thomas 1987: 76).

Third, people want permission to challenge the hypocrisy of the faith community, particularly where it says one thing and does another. Healthy dealing with conflict often means acknowledging and expressing anger, and the focus of this anger is often hypocrisy. Faith communities that cannot deal with anger can react in hypocritical ways. Kornfeld explores some of the reasons why this takes place:

> Many communities intend to be safe places where conflicts can be resolved, but they find conflict resolution difficult because so many of their members have difficulty expressing anger appropriately. Some members are afraid of their anger and cope with it by pushing it down or denying it. Others are . . . hijacked by it. They then feel picked up by rage and out of control. They lose their ability to think reasonably or act appropriately. They behave as if they are fighting for their lives . . . conflicts come from the unfinished business or unresolved, or poorly resolved, conflicts . . . When revered leaders leave, many members feel abandoned, angry, and in pain. Anger at the person who leaves sometimes goes underground and the hostility is taken out on the new leader . . . Another source of communal wounding comes from the community 'family secrets' about unacknowledged

or hidden pain in the congregation . . . the pain goes underground . . . Sometimes these secrets are about present activity, sometimes about past events that are still being lived out in the pain of those whose trust has been violated.

(1998: 24ff.)

Fourthly, people want permission to leave their faith community, without being labelled, scapegoated or punished for leaving (Douglas 1995), although this is often the response they encounter.

Phil was attending a community church that was charismatic in belief and practice. Coming from an Anglican background he found some of the change in style very freeing. His sense of worship grew and he found people warm and accepting. However, after a time Phil began to question different aspects of church life and raised these with other members of the small group he belonged to. After several weeks the leader asked him to stop his questioning as it was 'disruptive for the others and made them feel uncomfortable'. Phil complied, not wanting to upset anyone, but found that he could not stop questions from emerging. The next time he spoke, he was faced with a stony silence. His commitment to the group and the church began to waver and every so often he would go for a long walk on the local moors instead of attending church. A month later he was told that the leaders of the community wanted to see him. He felt excited as earlier in the year he had proposed a community art project and was waiting for the go-ahead from the leadership. But at the meeting he was questioned about his commitment and his unwillingness to accept discipline, and told that some would say that this was a 'rebellious spirit'. Phil felt attacked. This meeting threw him into emotional turmoil. How could people who had been so warm and accepting become so harsh? Over the next few months he attended irregularly, until he reached the point at which he could not carry on, and he left. He talked this over with friends and had a final meeting with the small group to explain his decision, almost seeking their permission. His hopes were dashed again as he was told bluntly that he had never really been part of them, being too influenced by being an Anglican, and that this had inoculated him against receiving true faith.

The same story could be told by others again and again. It is of course important that people take responsibility for their situation, even if this leads to painful choices.

> There comes the time when . . . some people feel the need to break away from their base group, to find for themselves an identity of their own; to wrestle with faith, philosophy or understanding which speaks to their experience . . . This breaking away is known by various names: religious symbols include the wilderness, the desert, the exile.
>
> (Jacobs 1993b: 6)

Fifth, some people want permission to let go of faith itself. In such situations the reality is that even if the pastor were to deny them permission to do this, it would make no difference to their intentions. But what a difference it might make if their reasons are understood, even if not agreed with by the pastoral helper. Some people need to work through an illusion of faith, and reach a point of disillusionment, where some may then discover 'God above God', 'religionless Christianity', 'the illusion beyond' (Jacobs 1993b: 21, 185); or 'in "transcendental moments" . . . in the immeasurably complex variety of the particulars of life, the symmetry of God' (Bomford 1999: 150).

> Psychotherapeutic theory teaches us the importance of helping people look at their conscious – and eventually their unconscious – conflicts so that they can be resolved . . . the therapist is a supportive, accepting presence who 'keeps the client company' while the conflict becomes clear . . . It is only after the client can *feel* the trouble that resolution can take place. Very often the conflict is resolved when its meaning is understood . . . both the client and therapist must learn patience.
>
> (Kornfeld 1998: 27)

What people are looking for in a pastoral context, as much as in the therapeutic context, is an advocate who will speak for them, and stand by them when they face the conflict that can arise from their needs, and the all too frequent clash that these have with the faith community's beliefs and values. This is a time-consuming process that cannot be rushed without losing something of the real depth and growth that conflict can promote in each of us. It requires the kind of faith that starts a journey and is not sure of the outcome.

The third route towards handling conflict is understanding power. Given the close relationship between power and sexuality, I examine this issue separately in the next chapter.

Chapter **13**

Conflicts of power and sexuality

Each of us is a sexual being with desires, drives, hopes, needs, fantasies and frustrations. The shape of my body, my knowledge of other bodies, the messages I have received, the memory of intimacy, the tender touch of pleasure, the lingering gaze, the longing for connection and the life-giving, beating heart of love all combine to make me the person I am. The Old Testament expresses these compelling aspects of our being human in the poetic words and images recorded in the Song of Solomon. I have described the powerful metaphor of the wounded healer in an earlier chapter; another potent metaphor is God as a wounded lover. 'That first blush of love when he found Israel, God said was like finding grapes in the desert. But as Israel broke his trust again and again, he was forced to endure the awful shame of the wounded lover . . . the powerful image of a jilted lover explains . . . the precise cycle of anger, grief, forgiveness, jealousy, love, pain that God himself went through' (Yancey 1995: 94). The image of God is of one who loves and suffers in ways that intimately describe the sexual nature of humanness. So it is another traumatic scar on the history of faith communities that they have often failed to hold together spirituality and sexuality in the way the Old Testament apparently does. Cotter writes 'Matters of sexuality and spirituality affect us all. Indeed, the sexual and the spiritual impulses may be the most significant, if not the most immediately powerful, in our lives' (1993: v).

Both Judaism and Christianity affirm the importance of an individual's *becoming* and believe that we are called by God to become ourselves . . . Buber quotes rabbi Yechiel Michal of Zloczov: It is the duty of every man in Israel to know and consider that in his nature he is unique in the world and that there has never been another like him. For had there been another like him, he would not need to be in the world. Each individual is a new thing in the world and must perfect his own nature in this world . . . by serving God in their own ways, in their own situations.

(Kornfeld 1998: 32ff.)

Human sexuality, then, is part of God-given uniqueness and it finds erotic, poetic and affectionate expression in sacred writings. These same writings also contain beliefs about the way sexuality is expressed. Traditionally this has focused on permanent marriage relationships for the physical, genital expression of sexuality and the procreation of children. Sex before marriage, outside marriage, with a family member or with a same-sex partner has been forbidden. Many of these prohibitions are challenged by the world in which we live. People who are single ask what they should do if they find celibacy is too difficult an option, given that they too have sexual feelings, and sexuality is such an important part of their humanness (Deshpande 2001). Sexuality and its physical expression is still a minefield for the faith community, despite the celebration of human uniqueness with its physical, spiritual, psychological and embodied dimensions (Cotter 1993: 14ff.).

But that is only one part, a neglected part, of the story. Sex and sexuality can also be taboo, shaming, forbidden, secret, furtive, guilt-laden, isolating, abusive, and exploitative of self and others. The context of our faith is a world that is charged with eroticism, experienced through a subculture – mainly to sell products where advertising is overwhelmed with sexual symbolism. We also see the devastating consequences of sexual freedom in the breakdown of relationships; there is an explosion of pornography, driven by the internet; the rate of teenage pregnancy is increasing; and the list goes depressingly on: the growth of sexually transmitted diseases; inexcusable homophobia; an appalling lack of intimacy; the fear of difference; the exploitation of the vulnerable living on the streets; and crushing statistics of sexual abuse at all levels. If ever we are tempted to have too optimistic a view of human nature, a quick survey of what people do to one another in the context of sex and sexuality is a sobering experience.

Stefan, a large, distinguished man, sat opposite me on the edge of his chair. I knew him by reputation as an imposing and charismatic speaker. His words tumbled out through heart-wrenching sobs, 'I just can't go on. There is nothing left; all I feel is despair.' He had called me as some-one recommended by a friend who had assured him I would listen and help. I sensed fear just below the surface, fear which soon overwhelmed his whole being. He confessed that he had never had much time for this 'counselling business' – it was for others who couldn't cope, while he got on with the real job. Stefan told me ashamedly that he had had an affair. His relationship with his wife had been strained for a long time and sex was no longer important in the marriage. It had come as a surprise that he had suddenly fallen head over heels in love with some-one he had met on a training course. In the course of a month he had gone from near celibacy to being a passionate lover. The strain of run-ning an illicit relationship, being in a conventional marriage, having a well-known public Christian profile and a demanding job had become too much. He knew from his faith perspective that he was doing wrong and had been shocked to discover that part of him did not want to let this woman go. He knew the pain he had caused his wife when she had found out, although she had been brave enough to recognize that she had a part to play in this complex scenario. What Stefan had not realized was that his wife had been in counselling for some time – which indicates the woeful level of communication in their marriage. She told him she had been able to find support from her counsellor, and this had helped Stefan realize that he might after all benefit himself.

What did Stefan want from me? Sometimes people in this situation are remorseful at getting 'caught out', but do not want to change and expect life to go on exactly as before. Others finding themselves in a similar position respond either by becoming cynical and abandoning faith altogether or coping through a gross over-identification with their faith position. Those who avoid either end of this spectrum often come to pastoral counsellors wanting the safety of confidentiality and a counselling relationship. Too often Christians find that when they have confided in Christian friends they have been badly let down. So, after telling his story and receiving neither condemnation nor absolution, what did Stefan want from me? He wanted to make sense of his life, in which sexuality and faith played important parts. I had to seek to answer with him the complex question of what Stefan needed. It emerged that he was afraid of intimacy. He needed a reparative attachment with someone who understood his faith background and was not taken in by it. Over the coming weeks we explored how his workaholic lifestyle was both helpful and unhelpful for the kingdom of God he so eloquently proclaimed. God undoubtedly used him; however, he was also very afraid of God. We discovered this by working on his fear of me, as a counsellor and what I represented. 'Wasn't Freud obsessed with sex?' he once asked. My reply was 'It wasn't Freud who was obsessed with sex, but maybe you could be.' Letting someone close enough sexually that they had power or control over him was a fearful thing, though less so as the counselling relationship progressed.

What links power and sexuality? Sexuality and spirituality are vital parts of being human and of our understanding of our identity. Sexuality and spirituality therefore have a profound impact on people's journey to find themselves, but they are also areas of immense vulnerability. They form part of our understanding of 'soul' and speak of the deepest aspect of our being. As we shall see later in this chapter, the abuse of power and sexuality leave deep, subconscious wounds, which may take a lifetime to explore and heal – even when healing is possible. In pastoral work in the area of sexuality, the abuse of power and the existence of sexual abuse in faith communities surfaces again and again.

The nature of power

Power and powerlessness are all around us, experienced by all of us, yet surprisingly difficult to define. Power has physical, philosophical, theological, sociological, political, racial and psychological dimensions, which make concise use of the word difficult. Storz helps by identifying the category of *power over*, meaning 'the desire to control, the ambition to dominate, the effort to enslave others and render the world subservient. She is talking about acting as though one were God' (quoted in Peters 1994: 98). Yet not all power is *power over*. Rollo May recognizes three categories of positive power: nutrient power; integrative power, and competitive power; and two further categories which equate with Storz's definition – manipulative power and exploitative power (quoted in Rayburn 1999: 893).

The pervasive and elusive nature of power make it all the more important to recognize and wrestle with it. Issues of power and powerlessness are always present in pastoral care and counselling: in the stories told by the person being helped, in the relationships both between helper and helped and between this pair and the faith community. A beneficial helping relationship mirrors a factor found to be helpful in therapeutic relationships, namely, the helper behaving 'as if he or she is someone who makes sense, who is worthy of attention, who has the power to choose and who has strengths' (McLeod 1998: 27). The power-enhancing dimension of a pastoral or therapeutic relationship can be enormously healing, but will often bring someone in a faith community into conflict over beliefs and values, as discussed in the previous chapter.

Power, like love and sexuality, has a seductive allure in subtle and varying ways.

Martin, a lay leader in a faith community, found it extremely difficult to come to terms with the end of his term of office. He became depressed and talked to his GP who was from a different faith tradition. The GP did not think that anti-depressants were the right solution and encouraged Martin to talk. As Martin was listened to he came to realize that he missed knowing what was going on, as he had become accustomed to doing. He thought of himself as the last person who would have clung to power, but he also had the self-awareness to see that the seeds were there in him. He came to see and understand that the power of the insider and of secret, privileged knowledge was addictive. Most people with knowledge of counselling skills find themselves carrying the secrets and burdens of others, and some may, like Martin, become addicted. But power, like the burdens and secrets which counsellors hear, needs to be handed back to the client. Empowering others is one of the marks of the great religious figures of world faiths.

The potential for pastoral care to give back power often leads to resistance on the part of leaders in faith communities. It is my observation that local clergy often resist using self-aware people within the pastoral life of a church. 'All I was allowed to do was visit the shut-up folk. Anyone who needed more than a chat over a cup of tea was deemed to be *his* province', said an experienced pastoral carer. There is a great need for faith community leaders to discover that their role need not be usurped if they allow another person with different skills to be involved. The competitive power recognized by May needs to be replaced by positive expressions of power: nutrient and integrative power. There is a vital role in faith contexts for suitably trained people with counselling skills. If ever the church, as a faith community, needed to change from being a monolithic structure with a hierarchical system of power enshrined in its tradition and beliefs, it is now. Whether future generations believe or cannot believe will be determined by the brave actions of those with responsibility and power at this present time.

The abuse of power in faith contexts

The abuse of power is hardly exclusive to faith contexts, and the worlds of counselling and psychotherapy still have much work to do in this area (Hetherington 1998, 2000a, 2000b). However, there is an implicit assumption that faith communities will be safe places for people in their vulnerability.

Nancy cried and cried. 'I never thought you would believe me', she stammered to her counsellor. 'After all you are a priest and a man at that. But I needed someone like you to hear me.' Gavin replied 'What was done to you was wrong, no matter whatever spiritual term it was given. It was wrong; and you should never have gone through that.' Nancy had escaped from a cult which used Christian terminology about 'rooting out sin' and 'sanctifying the flesh' to justify physical and sexual exploitation of group members through ritual flogging and humiliation. The scars of such abuse remained in her and in others who eventually escaped.

That may be an extreme example, but one of the positive aspects of the current wider social understanding of abuse is that those who are part of faith communities feel able to voice their concerns about unhealthy or harmful religion. A critique of the unhealthy aspects of religion or faith has been part of the psychoanalytic legacy and I shall not focus on those concerns here. However, I highlight the abuse of power as a fundamental aspect and a specific danger of any belief system that places great demands on those who follow it (Watts *et al.* 2002). Most spiritual abuse is not 'deliberately orchestrated by unscrupulous persons . . . it results from well-meaning, misguided or deluded authority figures' (Walker quoted in Layzell 1999: 112). Pattison argues that it is the nature of the religious institution that underpins the abuse of power. He terms it 'pastoral power'.

> Informal personal pressure or the threat of exposure and shame . . . is a manifestation of the kind of 'pastoral power' that Foucault identifies . . . Pastoral power . . . is orientated to the salvation of individual souls as well as to the whole Christian flock. In this context, individual obedience to the pastor is of vital importance. Significantly, the pastor must have total knowledge of each of his sheep: 'he must know what goes on in the soul of each one, that is, his secret sins' . . . Furthermore, 'this form of power cannot be exercised without knowing the insides of people's minds . . . making them reveal their innermost secrets' (Dreyfus and Rabinow 1982: 214) . . . Pastoral power was benevolent in intentions, panoptic in scope, and effective in inducing discipline, order and social control . . . It utilized the dynamics of guilt/forgiveness and shame/exclusion to maintain orthodoxy . . . Modern pastoral care may be less intrusive. However the exercise of pastoral and liturgical power still involves elements of guilt and shame, often unconsciously, to maintain obedience together with organisational unity, conformity and purity.
>
> (2000: 278)

I examine some issues of guilt and shame in the final chapter but an important expression of them is also found here. The potent combination of deep psychological need and unhealthy faith provide fertile soil for potentially abusive or harmful religion. The pastoral power inherent in the nature of faith communities should not be overlooked or underestimated. There is a vital role for people equipped with counselling skills and an awareness of faith matters, in helping individuals to explore the unseen aspects of their character, and in helping the faith community identify ways in which it is harming others. 'Detecting whether a person's Christian faith is unhelpfully intertwined with unmet psychological needs requires sensitive pastoral skills. It is only by getting to know a person quite deeply that we can begin to understand the meaning, and purpose, of religious beliefs and behaviours' (Watts *et al.* 2002: 61). There is a great need for places where people's voices can be heard and their stories told. Because religious abuse is often veiled in spiritual or theological terminology and liturgy, considerable listening skills are needed. It is important to hear what is being subtly hinted at, or sounds like a 'still small voice' in our emotional responses.

The pastoral listener also needs to be aware of the institution that may be unknowingly perpetrating abuse. It is perhaps most clearly seen in authoritarian or fundamentalist religious groups with a strong, usually male, leader. A dynamic develops in which such a person becomes inaccessible to all but an inner group, and those outside become negatively labelled. In the example given in Chapter 12, Phil was questioned about his apparent unwillingness to accept discipline and his 'rebellious spirit', when in fact all he was doing was expressing his normal, questioning self. Spiritual abuse can take place when 'an individual comes to represent or focus the malaise in a community . . . Because of who they were – female, pastorally sensitive, lay people, gay, vulnerable – or because of what they were noticing in the community, they became convenient scapegoats' (Layzell 1999: 114). Any large group, family, institution or community is capable of scapegoating others. Faith communities are no better and no worse than others (Douglas 1995: 70ff.), although they deserve more criticism given their aims of valuing and helping others, and the special nature of spiritual abuse. Spiritual abuse is that which takes place in a faith context or is done by a representative religious figure. It is found in all faiths although especially in those religious groups that many would view as cults. This specific context adds another layer of painful complexity to the abuse.

Because it is spiritual, the person suffers a spiritual wound. 'When a person is in a place of spiritual searching, she makes the deepest parts of herself vulnerable. To be wounded in these places is a very serious matter' (Layzell 1999: 112). 'If the spirit of a person can be damaged by the abusive or ill-informed actions of others, that same spirit may be soothed, healed or enabled to grow through careful, respectful and well-informed relationship' (Layzell 1999: 118). Here, then, is a clear task for the pastoral carer which calls upon all the counselling skills.

The nature of sexuality

Cotter, in trying to express what the word 'sexuality' means, gathers together different metaphors before concluding:

> Our sexuality then is full of intricacy and complexity. It is the stuff both of being stuck *and* of our growth in free-dom. Consequently, it is inevitably bound up with any-thing we may want to say about spirituality. Spirituality is nothing less than the whole of life orientated towards God, shaped by God, graced by God. That *includes* the sexuality of each individual and the sexuality of all, in our personal and corporate desire to come together and to create.
>
> (1993: 5)

Sexuality is an elusive and complex subject, which has often been treated in a simplistic way by faith communities. Within such communities there are some for whom it is vital that there is a clear-cut distinction between right and wrong, good and bad, sinner and saint, with defined codes of behaviour. For such people the suggestion that, for example, masturbation is a normal part of sexual expression would be blasphemous. To suggest shades of grey or add new colours profoundly disturbs their black and white world. Yet within the same faith communities there are those who are able to hold the paradoxes concerning sexuality outlined by Cotter. Given such a faith context, how can pastoral carers meet sexuality as they encounter it in those they help? It is useful to identify four particular areas.

Awareness and acceptance of our own feelings about sexuality

Sex is not a split-off part of self, untouched by those we encounter. Orbach begins the opening chapter of her book *The Impossibility of Sex* with the words 'I felt twitches in my vagina, pleasurable contractions' (1999: 7). Her book gives a real sense of what psychotherapy is about, yet when I was talking to a Christian group of pastoral carers I told them not to be put off by the opening words. Why? What was I ashamed of? Was I protecting them or myself? Reflecting on it I realized that I and perhaps many others have hesitant feelings about their own bodies and sexuality. Yet if we cannot deal with our own sexuality, we are less likely to be able to hear another's sexual story. Kirk and Leary write that

> the combination of both clinical and research findings . . . strongly suggests that many clergy are ill at ease with their sexuality, have not resolved issues from childhood relating to gender, struggle with the church's ambivalence on sex, find it difficult to communicate on emotional or sexual matters, and often have problems with their marriage stemming from these factors.
>
> (1994: 98)

An associated issue is that of embodiment. How we feel about our physical body has great bearing on our feelings about our sexuality. So often sexuality and physical attractiveness are equated and celebrated in celluloid, with no mention of cellulite. Janet Morley (1992: 113) describes this paradox in her poem 'The Bodies of Grownups':

> The bodies of grownups
> come with stretchmarks and scars,
> faces that have been lived in,
> relaxed bellies and breasts,
> backs that give trouble,
> and well-worn feet:
> flesh that is particular,
> and obviously mortal.
> They also come

with bruises on their heart,
wounds they can't forget,
and each of them
a company of lovers in their soul
who will not return
and cannot be erased.
And yet I think there is a flood of beauty
beyond the smoothness of youth;
and my heart aches for that grace of longing
that flows through bodies
no longer straining to be innocent
but yearning for redemption.

Morley captures spirituality, sexuality and embodiment in a tender way. In doing so she sets a good example for pastoral carers. The challenge in helping others begins with helping oneself. A high degree of self-awareness is required if we are genuinely to help others in the area of sexuality. The Jewish perspective on sexuality appears healthier by contrast, precisely because of a more embodied tradition.

It emphasizes neither the exaggeration of nor aversion to sex, and considers sex to be neither evil nor base. Neither is sex in itself the magical key to all meaning and fulfilment, though it is profound in its spiritual significance. Rather sex is regarded as essential for cementing a healthy relationship between husband and wife. It requires education, tact and modesty and is to be approached in a natural and wholesome way, yet controlled by self-discipline.

(Brayer 1990: 1159)

Much of the work that a Jewish pastoral counsellor does in that faith context concerns sex, sexuality, marriage, family and children. The Jewish tradition then finds a wider expression and place for sexuality that is a good model for other faith traditions to follow – although there is still considerable debate within the Jewish community, which represents a split between orthodox and liberal interpretations of the Torah.

An ability to hear the real issue

A pastoral carer who has developed good listening skills may be told painful and sad stories concerning sexuality, about which the person does not feel they can talk to his or her faith leader. As one woman put it, 'How can you comfortably sit in a service week by week when you have confessed to the church leader the affairs that no one else knows about? I flinch inside when certain Bible passages are mentioned and hear hypocritical echoes in my head. Everyone thinks we have the perfect marriage; but the real truth is that he is a bully, a coward who resorts to fists wrapped in a towel so the bruises won't show. I know why I fall for other men: they show me love, affection; and before I know it, it's all gone too far. Really it's revenge, pay-back time, for all those punches that didn't leave marks on the outside. I know where to hit him where it really hurts.' It was not therefore sexuality that was the real issue for this woman, though someone working from a prescriptive faith position might have assumed that from the fact that she had had several affairs. When she was given the space to talk, it became clear that sexuality was only one aspect of a much more complex, tangled and painful story. Her affairs were a way of avoiding the fear of being abandoned if she left the marriage, which is what she really wanted to do (Kornfeld 1998: 249).

The issue of inclusion versus exclusion

The challenge posed by homosexual and lesbian sexualities for faith communities is one of the major debates, if not quite the unspoken test of orthodoxy in current theological debates (Rogers 1999: 26). A decade ago I joined a group of theological researchers. I was the only new person in the group and I was not introduced or acknowledged in any way. The theological debate was on a specialist area of which I had little knowledge. I felt myself becoming more and more angry; and rather than address the issue and express my feelings to others, I simply resolved that I would never go back. I felt excluded even though I had been specially invited. There was no introductory welcome recognizing me as an individual, or any use of an inclusive language that facilitated someone like me less sure of the vocabulary or meanings.

That gave me an insight into what it means to feel excluded. It helped me understand what exclusion feels like from the inside out, and threw light on how I might address the issue of homosexuality. The challenge for a faith community is whether it wants to be an inclusive community open to all, whatever their sexual orientation, or whether it is to continue as it is, predominantly an exclusive community. To become an inclusive community requires willingness to change – something that many faith communities find very difficult. Given that they span a huge cross-section of people, faith communities hold within them a diversity of opinion, but they are often ruled by a consensus view, which operates at the level of the lowest common denominator. It is important such faith communities should hear the voice of those who possess pastoral sensitivity and insight, so that they can embrace an inclusive approach to all people, whatever their sexuality, or indeed any other fundamental aspect which could otherwise separate them from the majority.

The challenge of honesty and acceptance

It is easy to accept someone in theory, but when we are face to face with some people we discover how feelings affect us as much as our ideas. It is also easier to hold beliefs when they are not challenged by real people and their situations.

The issue of homosexuality confronts Christians with difficult choices. Pierson writes with real concern for the pastoral care of homosexual Christians (1989) and Hallett writes about sexual identity and the choice of celibacy as an act of discipleship (1997). Similarly Townsend concludes,

> Homosexual behaviour can only be affirmed by Christians if the following are accepted: the repudiation of a created moral order, a shift from objective to subjective morality, and a new centre of gravity in theology whereby human insights and 'pastoral' concerns can take precedence over divine revelation.
>
> (1994: 4)

On the other hand Vasey challenges,

> 'You have neglected the more important matters of the law – justice, mercy and truthfulness. These you should have practised' (Matt. 23:23) . . . Christians have a responsibility to work for a more just social order and to look to the interests of those who are abused and misrepresented in society. Four factors sharpen this imperative to stand with gay people in their search for justice . . . Firstly, many gay people are Christians . . . Secondly, the scriptures have been misused to support a climate in which gay people are feared . . . Thirdly, Christians have contributed to an atmosphere of hostility towards gay people . . . Fourthly, the Gospel of Jesus Christ is itself obscured by the alienation of the church from gay people.
>
> (1991: 23)

Townsend is right: human insights and pastoral concerns have found an increasingly authoritative voice. But they have not replaced divine revelation. Rather they represent the development of a new pastoral hermeneutic that genuinely listens to the narratives of people as well as the narrative of God. As Bartholemew puts it, 'Hermeneutics is just a sophisticated word for knowing better how to listen to the text so as to hear properly what God is saying to his people, at this time and in this place' (2002: 13). Not all faith communities have reacted negatively to this issue: although the research is dated (as attitudes to homosexuality have changed markedly in the last decade), those from the Jewish faith have shown a less negative response to accepting homosexuality than any other religious group surveyed (Beit-Hallahmi and Argyle 1997: 205).

The following is the story of one such person and her struggle with honesty and acceptance as she works towards a new pastoral hermeneutic.

> I remember the anger – indeed rage – I felt during confrontations with my friends in the healing ministry. It could all have ended in bitter recriminations and separation. However, we had been on this road together for eight years and decided to hold on to what we had in common and to keep

talking. We still disagree over the gay issue but are able to love and respect one another and enjoy a very real friendship. This is because of honest communication. In contrast, I have just resigned from leadership in a church where such honesty did not exist and it became impossible to function in an authentic manner.

(Burns 2002: 5)

The pastoral carer will therefore be faced with uncomfortable and challenging issues related to sexuality. There are no easy answers, although there are too many false dichotomies and there is an overpowering temptation to sit on the fence. My own conviction is that people who are vulnerable about the response to their sexuality demand more from us.

The abuse of sexuality

The reality of sexual abuse is an inescapable fact of life that society has long denied, but has come to accept in the last fifteen years. I have worked as a counsellor in and outside the church, and I do not believe that sexual abuse is any better or any worse in faith communities or its leaders. Therapists also sexually abuse clients, as Hetherington writes:

Therapy entails a private and intimate encounter most often between opposite-sex dyads and as such provides a suitable environment for sexual abuse. The client's perceptions of the safety of the encounter and the trusting relationship may further fuel the desires of those therapists who have a proclivity to abuse.

(1998: 363)

It is this that makes a link with the issue of power in faith communities. But if abuse can happen in any power relationship, it still needs recognizing and facing by and within faith communities.

Among faith community leaders

Although research is limited and based on a small number of studies in the USA, figures show that 37 per cent of clergy said they had engaged in inappropriate sexual behaviour, but not necessarily with members of their congregation. These figures are higher than comparable groups but have probably been influenced by the culture of honest reporting (Watts *et al.* 2002: 261). Kornfeld adds,

> I have found among the seminary students I have taught a higher incidence of childhood physical, emotional and sexual abuse. My students, who were in the process of healing, were drawn to ministry as 'wounded healers'. In many instances, belief in a loving God was the lifeline they grasped as children in the terror of their abuse. Others were in seminary to find or come to terms with the God whom they felt let them down in the nightmare of their childhood . . . Caregivers whose wounds have been healed can use their experience . . . those who are still in denial of their own abuse are often unable to hear or believe those who come for counsel and referral.
>
> (1998: 257)

Such faith leaders may use the community to meet their own needs, burdened as they are by an open wound or wounds. Those in denial or who are still traumatized may find that they become part of a collusive leadership that does not name abuse when it happens. Some church communities cover up allegations of abuse. There have been instances when pastoral carers within a community have established that a church leader was abusing his position by fondling and touching women but when they raised this with the other leaders they have been accused of doing the devil's work in defaming the character of a man of God, and have been asked to leave. It is possible for whole congregations to use denial as a defence against the unthinkable, and to be unable to acknowledge that it might actually be true. Yet the damage done in a faith community can have far-reaching impact that can take years, if not decades, to heal.

Among faith community members

Just as there may be a proportion of faith leaders carrying the scars of abuse there are an even greater number of faith community members who have experienced sexual abuse. It is difficult to know what proportion this is, but it needs to be borne in mind when looking at the way the community expresses its life and worship. The most obvious difficulty for women abused by fathers is the traditional way of addressing God as Father in most Christian congregations. The use of inclusive language and an ability to address God in male and female terms is not just political correctness gone mad. Such sensitivity is necessary in so many ways. For instance, in a typical congregation we might find one woman who is single, terrified of, but longing for, opposite-sex relationship. Her traumatic state is related to her rape as a teenager. Another is increasingly annoyed by the faith community's focus on families, and the exclusion of other relationships. In her case internal damage following childhood abuse makes it impossible for her to have a family. There is a man who was abused by a neighbour, a family friend who used to take him swimming as neither his parents could swim. It was all very exciting until he started his 'special lessons'. Or there may be another member of the congregation who was ritually abused by an 'uncle' without her parents ever knowing, and who has subsequently experienced the discomforting experience of multiple personalities. Or there is a man who was abused by an older sibling – a form of abuse that is probably more widespread than has traditionally been realized. These people are part of what appears to be a 'normal' congregation, yet it contains a number of stories of abuse that are unspoken, and others that are yet to be remembered. What such stories tell us is that there needs to be some awareness training about abuse in faith communities. A good example is the Baptist denomination's encouragement for each church to offer training in this area, through its 'Safe to Grow' policy and the accompanying resource book (Baptist Union 2002).

As encountered by pastoral carers

Many of the people described in the section above told their stories to pastoral carers. Of course, abuse is a complex area and it usually requires specialist counselling help with appropriate supervision. It can be a difficult issue to contain within a faith community, especially when someone who has been badly damaged wants to hit out. Yet at the point where the pastoral carer is told such history and before referral can even be thought about, there is a right and a wrong way to respond. Draucker (1992: 30) gives examples of helpful and unhelpful responses. Non-helpful responses include:

> 'Oh, my God. I can't believe anyone could actually do anything that horrible to a child. What your father did was disgusting.' (shock)

> 'It sounds like you believe your father did these things to you. You were so young, it is hard to know what really happened.' (disbelief)

> 'Why did you agree to have sex with him? Why did you not tell your mother? Why did it go on for so long?' (blaming)

> 'You say that this experience is in the past and that you've coped with it. Why don't we move on then to the concerns you have today?' (minimizing)

> 'Tell me exactly what he did to you sexually.' (voyeuristic)

More helpful responses include:

> 'I am concerned about the experience you shared with me; I wonder if you want to tell me more about it. Sexual abuse can be a very painful experience for children, and can continue to have an impact on one's life as an adult.' (showing calm concern without showing disgust)

> 'I can imagine it was hard for you to share that experience with me. I respect your courage for being able to do so.' (acknowledging difficulty of disclosure)

> 'It can be very important to discuss your sexual abuse

experience as so often it is related to your current concerns. However, we can do this at a pace that feels right to you.' (reinforcing client's control of disclosure process)

'For some people, sharing an abuse experience for the first time can result in some very distressing feelings. How are you feeling now? ... Do you feel unsafe in any way?' (acknowledging feelings, assessing safety)

More detailed explorations of abuse are helpfully and sensitively dealt with by Walker in *Surviving Secrets* (1992). Abuse that takes place in a spiritual or religious setting may be even more complicated. If there are elements of ritual abuse or cult-based abuse, specialist help is necessary, although not always easy to find (Mollon 1996). Layzell's deceptively simple chapter on 'Pastoral Counselling with Those Who Have Experienced Abuse in Religious Settings' is also very helpful (Lynch 1999).

This chapter has come a long way from its initial focus on spirituality and sexuality. Despite the seriousness of the last section, it is important not to lose sight of the vision of sexuality and spirituality joining in ways that make people whole. Cotter writes:

> Our sexuality is fundamental to our lives, both through delight and contradiction. The further we pursue the questions which are raised by our sexuality, the more we are made aware of the profoundest movements of our being. Through our experiences of sexuality there is the possibility of our becoming more open to the Beyond whom we call God.
>
> (1993: 5)

The quality of pastoral care people receive in this area especially can make an enormous difference to their quality of life and the ongoing health of the faith community.

Chapter **14**

Conflicts with guilt, shame and forgiveness

Guilt

> Lizzie was a young single parent who brought her toddler along to a church-based group. At first she was very defensive in my attempts to talk with her and stared at me with hostility. Over the year Lizzie talked more openly about her life and her struggles and then one day she appeared at church when I was preaching on an evangelistic theme. I recall thinking about how opportune a moment this was as I explained about the way we sin and what God has done about this. Before the service had finished Lizzie left in tears and I never saw her again. As I reflected on this I could see clearly how much it had cost Lizzie to take this step of coming to church; but in my evangelistic zeal to rescue, I lost the compassion that she had encountered in me that made her take that brave step in the first place.

I still experience pangs of guilt about this. The guilt concerns my view of myself as someone who cares – my own personal code of the kind of person I want to be and how I respond to others. I think I let Lizzie down, and myself. Guilt appears to be a universal phenomenon found in all writings, religious and classical. Shakespeare's most haunting play opens with witches, sees the death of a king, records the appearance of a ghost, and ends with madness, despair and death. Throughout it the guilt felt by Macbeth touches the tragic aspects of life, yet the haunting portrayal of the destructive power of guilt reaches its zenith in the crazed figure of Lady Macbeth. The full range of guilt finds echoes in our own heart and soul, illustrating that guilt is a fairly universal phenomenon, except perhaps in certain anti-social or psychopathic personalities (Oates 1990: 46). It is also a central religious concept, and is likely therefore to form an important part of pastoral care and counselling.

The task of helping others with their guilt can be understood as a three-stage process:

- locating the particular form of guilt;
- assessing the function guilt plays; and
- accepting both the person and his or her guilt.

The form of guilt

There are as many forms and descriptions of guilt as there are hours in a day. Different authors have categorized it in various ways, yet there is something elusive and enmeshing about guilt that even profoundly insightful people, like Freud, failed to address (Strozier 1997: 167). It has a paralysing presence in the helping relationship, and a clue to its presence is often when there is a 'stuck' quality to the work, where the usual counselling skills seem to be dulled in their impact. 'Guilt can be a perplexing and uncomfortable feeling. Held inside the individual it corrodes good feelings. Expelled outside, it often confuses those who receive it' (Orbach 1994: 205). To add another layer of complexity, guilt is often linked to religion. Billy Connolly, the Scottish comedian, remarked 'I was brought up in Partick (in Glasgow) as a Catholic. The only qualification I got was an A level in guilt.' As usual, humour also speaks the truth that for many people religion has been experienced as a list of rules and regulations – rather than as a living relationship – using guilt as a means of moral or emotional control. However, Coltart offers another religious perspective:

> Guilt is fundamental to Judaism and Christianity, and there-
> fore strongly permeates Western culture and psychological

development. All therapists, whatever their orientation, know that guilt, both conscious and unconscious, is at the heart of much Western psychopathology. A considerable amount of therapeutic ingenuity is devoted to disentangling and eliminating neurotic guilt ... Elimination of guilt through peace of mind; drives to reparation and expiation often have to be satisfied in compensation for the preceding or not fully resolved guilt-feelings. In Buddhist psychology, since guilt is only one of many transient emotions ... there is far less masochistic addiction to self-blame ... In place of the massive psychic structures occupied by neurotic guilt ... Buddhist psychology ... speaks not of 'sins', or sources of guilt, but of what are called 'hindrances'.

(1993: 112ff.)

Coltart's perspective is helpful. It forces us to consider another viewpoint, whilst recognizing the huge presence guilt has within culture and the human psyche. Yet she does not answer the question of what this guilt is, that is so ever present and powerful. The following summaries are ways in which guilt has been described and demonstrate its wide-ranging influence.

Transgression or true guilt   People feel guilty when they have done something wrong that contravenes a moral, religious or legal code. Wrongdoing has occurred and the guilt is justified. A car driver who kills or injures another when driving over the legal alcohol limit is rightly guilty of breaking the law for which there is a penalty; and is morally guilty of harm to others.

Irrational, neurotic, false or subjective guilt   (Stein 1990: 488ff.) This is the opposite of normal guilt: neurotic, false or subjective guilt is 'disproportionate to the wrong committed, may induce repression, and is often accompanied by anxiety' (Narramore 1984: 105ff.). It is not based in an external reality and can become an elusive aspect of working with someone. People's experience of guilt is not always logical.

Andrew, a church member, caused the death of a pedestrian who had stepped out in front of his car. The accident could not have been avoided and Andrew was not blamed. He felt very guilty about this, yet never evidenced the slightest guilt over the sexual and physical abuse that he perpetrated on his daughter. His way of dealing with the guilt of the accident may have been rooted in the unacknowledged guilt of the sexual abuse. There was no rational connection apparent to others at the time, as the abuse of his daughter was not disclosed until much later.

There are also people who want help precisely because their experience of guilt is irrational and they cannot find a reason. As I show later, this is best dealt with through the quality of the helping relationship. Talking with someone who has the relevant counselling skills and awareness of a faith community context can help people explore what the guilt means for them and what it may say about their past. Where this takes the form of obsessional guilt, often involving rituals, specialist help is called for.

Perfection guilt   A common feature of this form of guilt is that the person does not feel good enough. Despite great effort they can never 'attain impossibly high levels set for them by perfectionist parents, teachers and church leaders' (Gordon 2000: 5). It may well be that this form of guilt is the root of the irrational guilt just mentioned. It possibly represents a form of shame at not living up to what analysts call the 'ego-ideal'.

Rejection guilt   The way some people are treated leads them to believe that they are bad people, because only bad people could feel this level of guilt. 'They have suffered serious rejection, marked by emotional deprivation and verbal and physical abuse' (Gordon 2000: 5). Sexual abuse needs specific mention here, as 82 per cent of women blame themselves for the abuse taking place (Sanderson 1995: 58). This is sometimes inculcated in them by the abuser who tells them how bad they are.

Survivor guilt   Victims of the Holocaust, both first and second generation (Bettelheim 1979: 29ff; Kogan 1995: 17), survivors of torture (Pokorny 1988: 91) and those who have experienced trauma can feel a profound sense of guilt about having survived when others did not. The presence of such guilt is one of the DSM IV (Diagnostic and Statistical Manual: American Psychiatric Association) criteria for post-traumatic stress disorder (Hetherington 2001: 20, 42, 67ff.).

Legal guilt   If I drive past a speed camera, it flashes and a fine arrives in the post, I am legally guilty of breaking a speed limit and must pay the penalty. There is objective evidence that forms the basis of the guilt. However, because nobody is apparently hurt by this process there is often little or no guilt experienced. On the other hand, if I lost my licence and my job as a result, the consequences for my family would cause a good degree of guilt. This form of guilt is the most straightforward to deal with as it can be acknowledged and owned, even if it is uncomfortable. It tells us that we have caused hurt to another and recognizes the hurt we have caused to ourselves. But when acceptance and reparation do not ease the guilt, then it may have links to irrational guilt.

Existential or ontological guilt   Buber uses this term to refer to the broader social, community and religious dimensions of an individual's actions. This 'occurs when someone injures an order of the human world whose foundations he knows and recognises as those of his own existence and of all human existence' (Stein 1990: 490; see also Atkinson 1995: 425; Pattison 2000: 7).

Culturally located guilt   The nature of this form of guilt relates to the acceptance of a reality or standard by which conduct is measured, and which is culturally specific. What may not be a guilty action for one person might incur guilt for someone who has a different set of cultural norms, which may arise from their faith community. For example, a Jew marrying someone outside the faith incurs guilt because his or her belief system forbids it; this was the key issue found in one US study of problems taken to rabbis and Jewish counsellors. Such guilt is sometimes related to religious codes, but of little relevance to the secular population. But a more secular example relates to gender. ' "Show me a woman who isn't guilty and I'll show you a man." Although Erica Jong wrote this phrase well over a decade ago, guilt remains a disabling emotional response in many women's lives' (Orbach 1994: 205). Orbach identifies the huge demands women face as a source of guilt that leaves women feeling scolded, suffocated, stuck, glued, paralysed, silenced, anxious and angry.

Internalized or introjected guilt 'There is an intricate process of inter-personal and intra-personal interaction involving one's own wishes and desires, the desires of others, and the emotions of respect, love, envy, fear and anger that together shape a child's conscience and proneness to guilt' (Narramore 1984: 238). Even if a person's faith develops and moves beyond dependence on a religious system there can still be 'persistent "niggles" of guilt, as though in their liberation they had been more successful at overthrowing external authority, than in dealing adequately with internal authority-figures who continue to needle their conscience' (Jacobs 1993b: 134).

Intrinsic guilt This is a term used almost exclusively by the humanistic writer Maslow. By it he meant a 'betrayal of one's own inner nature of self, a turning off the path of self-actualization and ... essentially qualified self-disapproval' (quoted in Narramore 1984: 153). This has some similarities to existential guilt.

Developmental guilt Not all guilt is negative. It plays an important part in healthy emotional development and in learning to care for others, leading to reparation, concepts first developed by Melanie Klein (Jacobs 1993b: 139). The presence of such guilt is not pathological and can, as Klein suggests, lead to a desire to make reparation or to care for others. It does therefore have a healthy function to play in psychological development. Winnicott talks about guilt as joined 'on one hand to destructiveness and on the other hand to constructive activity' (1986: 81). A therapeutic understanding of guilt enables people to recognize their love and their hate, their anger and their loss, their hope and their fear. In health we are often ambivalent about many issues, not denying the negative aspects of self. It is nevertheless difficult to identify just what sort of guilt most people are experiencing, since often more than one form of guilt is present. Since the use of counselling skills helps a story to be told, reasons for guilt may become clearer in the course of telling it.

The function of guilt

As the first and the last categories above show, guilt is not all bad. It locates us in a world of codes, beliefs, rules and values, which also find expression in faith communities. Guilt has an important place in the spiritual and social dimensions of being human. It 'alerts us to the importance of paying attention to the effects of an ill-conceived action . . . we can find a way to accept our behaviour, to understand our actions and their implications' (Orbach 1994: 206). It locates us in a relational context.

> A person's whole emotional life . . . is determined by the state of these long term, committed relationships. As long as these are running smoothly he is content; when they are threatened he is anxious and perhaps angry; when he has endangered them by his own actions he feels guilt; when they are broken he feels sad; and when they are resumed he is joyful.
>
> (Bowlby 1988: 80)

Guilt also brings about recognition and understanding of the nature of ambivalence, and this is a crucial part both of therapeutic work and of faith development (Narramore 1984: 253ff.; Jacobs 1993b: 138).

However, the concept of guilt can be misused, perhaps most commonly when people in authority try to manipulate others. Faith communities are particularly prone to using guilt in this manipulative way, although I have noticed it in the voluntary sector and other charitable organizations as well. Another misuse of guilt is when it is experienced for good reason, but does not lead to change. In churches people can feel guilty about certain situations that they do not do anything to resolve or help. It is as if they think that it is enough to feel guilty, and that this absolves them from any action, challenge or change. Perhaps this is an effect of the overuse of guilt as a motivating factor. This response to guilt may need the challenging skills of the middle stage of the helping skills model.

Accepting the person and his or her guilt

Acceptance, as I described in Chapter 5, is a crucial quality that is important in all relationships, but it is especially important in the presence of guilt and shame. By accepting a person and using the relevant counselling skills, this

> encourages the patient to talk as freely as possible and enables the analyst to pay attention without distraction. A crucial element in the patient's ability to express himself openly is freedom from guilt. Many of those who seek therapy are, consciously or unconsciously, wracked by guilt.
>
> (Lomas 1993: 40)

Gordon's doctoral research on guilt identifies acceptance as coming from four main sources:

- caring professionals who are good listeners, understanding, non-judgmental and encouraging;
- supportive relatives and friends who exhibit the same characteristics;
- balanced Christianity – credal convictions and community life, which emphasize grace as well as law, and which advocate openness to people with all their faults, limitations and hurts;
- (less commonly) an individual who, through special skill or insight, is able to make precisely relevant – and therefore liberating – pronouncements.

> (2000: 5)

Working with guilt is a progressive process. People can find the courage to change and to let go of habitual patterns or responses, if they feel accepted. Then they can enter into a new level of awareness and possibly of healing.

The healing process requires recognition of the type of guilt or shame, a response appropriate to that type, and the presence of someone who embodies and demonstrates the qualities of forgiveness, affirmation and welcome. But because the process is not one-sided, there is a parallel need, on the part of those who feel guilty, for genuine repentance when it is appropriately called for; or the adoption of realistic standards by the perfectionist; or willingness on the part of the rejected to trust those who offer friendship and support. When helper and sufferer work together in this way then the alleviation of guilt feelings becomes possible (Gordon 2000: 5).

Shame

There are clear links between guilt and shame, although Patton suggests that shame may in some circumstances be an even more painful feeling:

> Christianity and pastoral carers have a vested interest in maintaining the primacy of guilt because it is easier to understand, can be dealt with at a cognitive level, seems to require an immediate, quick, verbal response such as confession or catharsis, and allows pastors to feel some measure of power and control. They can do something instantly like pronouncing absolution instead of feeling powerless, even ashamed.
>
> (Quoted in Pattison 2000: 199)

Dealing with shame therefore means entering into the shame and pain of others and this cannot be done lightly. It is interesting that shame has until recently played a surprisingly small part in the literature of pastoral care and counselling (Lomas 1993: 149). In guilt the focus is on what we do or have done, whereas in shame the focus is on who we are and what has been done to us. To be shamed is to experience an attack (by others or from within ourselves) on our very being as a person. It is 'a painful feeling of being exposed, uncovered, unprotected, vulnerable' (Schneider 1990: 1160). Yet shame also has an ability to silence, as it touches deep wounds and places of powerlessness.

Most people who have helped others have encountered, felt and borne the shame of another. There is something invasive and abusive about it. As the recognition of sexual abuse has grown over the last decade this may account for the new focus on the subject that finds its culmination in Pattison's book

Shame (2000). He combines profound personal insight with stimulating social, psychological and theological analysis and exposition. If we can offer any help to others it is by letting shame have a voice. Yet before we can do that we need to become aware of the shame that is within us, otherwise we will not be able to hear others with the clarity and compassion they deserve. Pattison counsels,

> Know thyself! Shame is a category of hiddenness, wordless-ness, abomination and rejection. It is difficult, and may be literally appalling, to become aware of its presence and effects. However without this kind of awareness it is difficult to see how progress can be made. If dysfunctionally or chronically shamed lives are lived out without any conscious knowledge of the effects of shame in them, shame may be passed on to or replicated in others ... A first practical response must, therefore, be to make some attempt to understand the shadow of shame in one's own life.
>
> (2000: 290)

Even if one develops this degree of self-awareness and knowledge of one's own shame, dealing with it is no easy task. Mollon explains why:

> Shame is inherent in sexual abuse. Indeed sexual abuse is the ultimate shame ... By definition we are talking of intensely private, intimate and shameful experiences. If the abuse has not been private but has involved several abusers in a network of paedophiles or a cult, then the shame and humiliation are intensified. The natural privacy of the self has been violated and autonomy has been mocked. The reaction is to want to hide the abuse. Shame is for the self and for the connection to the abuser.
>
> Shame is the hidden affect. Shame gives rise to shame about shame. Shame is contagious. If we connect empathically with another's shame we feel shame. Not surprisingly, both patients and therapists have tried to avoid contact with shame, preferring instead to focus on feelings of guilt, aggression and sadism – all of which can be fuelled by shame ... The affect of shame tends to block empathy.

Therapists do not want to feel this most toxic of emotions ... If we empathise with the abused patient we experience shame vicariously ... However there is another means by which we may be forced to experience shame ... When struggling against the shameful state of victimhood the patient may place the therapist in the role of the abused and shame-ridden victim.

(1996: 55)

The level of therapeutic skill that Mollon describes is usually beyond that of the pastoral helper or even the trained counsellor. Specific psychotherapy is needed to contain the shame and hold the boundary issues that are likely to emerge. What the pastoral helper can do is support the person within the faith community, while he or she is doing most therapeutic work elsewhere. Yet even here there is a danger that we dare not to listen to that person's story as a friend, companion or pastoral helper, because we do not want to experience his or her shame or encounter again its painful echoes in our own life. If people are silenced by their shame, their voice needs to be heard and their story told (Layzell 1999: 118ff.). Orbach addresses the issue of how to deal with guilt, but speaks also for those experiencing shame:

The person feels trapped and can't envisage a way out. If that guilt can be seen as a trap then questions can be asked about its function. In raising questions, we have the possibility of thinking about our options differently. If guilt is seen as the beginning of a response rather than an end point then it need not be so crippling. It can open up new ways of relating to entrenched patterns and ways of being.

(1994: 208)

Shame also raises huge questions for Christian theology, and here again Pattison's words might be heeded – that we talk theology as a way of avoiding the shame in us and others, by trying to add some theoretical gloss. Some believe that the death of Christ, as an example of sacrificial love, is able to transform personhood and 'has a particular resonance for those whose predominant emotion is shame' (Watts *et al.* 2002: 292). More than that, it is possible that 'some shame is appropriate', as we encounter God in whose presence we may feel ashamed, although we are not shamed by Him. Goodliff suggests that healing can be found through visual iconography, by a meditation and gaze on the face of Christ, who bears our shame and the shame of others as sacrifice. Watts *et al.* assert that when we feel ashamed in front of other people, it is often because we can sense they can see through us, and that there are no defences left against their critical gaze. Although God can see through us, and there are no more places to hide from Him, His gaze is a benevolent one. The critical gaze of God thus has a different effect (Watts *et al.* 2002: 12). Others are not as prescriptive or as optimistic as this, believing that theology has huge challenges to face if its voice is to be heard in the shame-filled lives of many people, inside and outside faith communities (Pattison 2000: 248, 296ff.).

Forgiveness

Theological questions about guilt and shame also raise the equally complex subject of forgiveness. What does the word forgiveness mean? In the first place, forgiveness is always relational. It is the recognition that something has gone wrong in a relationship. It also indicates a refusal to let what is wrong stop reconciliation, restoration or reparation taking place. It is of course a central belief in the many world faiths and one that finds expression in liturgies and rituals. For the Christian the key phrase is 'Forgive us our sins as we forgive those that sin against us', part of the Lord's Prayer that is in constant use (Bridger and Atkinson 1994: 204). But while it is relatively easy to talk about forgiveness in theoretical or theological terms it is much more complex in practice. Müller-Fahrenholz, a German theologian, writes:

> How dare I as a German talk about forgiveness? Fifty years have passed since the Nazis committed their atrocities against the Jewish people in Europe . . . against members of opposition parties, religious activists and many other persons considered 'unfit' for life . . . The more consciously I have moved along this road of hurt and shame . . . the more I have been driven to the conclusion that it is necessary to

think about forgiveness not *in spite of* Auschwitz but *because of* Auschwitz.

(Müller-Fahrenholz 1997: vi)

Müller-Fahrenholz gives six reasons why 'contemplating the meaning of forgiveness in the light of the furnaces of Auschwitz' requires the finding of new perspectives.

- Forgiveness is a crucial issue for the perpetrator and the victim.
- Hurt and shame get passed on from one generation to another, consciously and unconsciously.
- Guilt and shame have collective dimensions and cannot simply be reduced to an individual level.
- Forgiveness can never be an alternative to justice. 'Forgiveness is about renouncing unjustified power, not about weakening the pursuit of justice.'
- Forgiveness also needs to go beyond justice and include 'restitution of the human'.
- Forgiveness faces us with a paradox. 'The quest for what is truly human transcends the human race.'

(1997: viii–xi)

Forgiveness, guilt, shame and healing are bound together in a way that makes it possible for victims or perpetrators, whether for first, second or third generations or at collective, tribal, societal or national levels, to encounter 'new and constructive alliances'. This cannot be done on our own and Müller-Fahrenholz's answer is as follows:

> There will be and must be many answers to these questions ... rooted in a part of the Jewish and Christian traditions which is shared by Islam. The holy scriptures of the Abrahamite religions insist that the human-ness of the human race is grounded in the mercy of God. As we work for forgiveness, we are called to reflect that as human beings each of us is created in the image of God, the Most Merciful. This is our calling and mission: to become mirrors of mercy.

(1997: xi)

I warm to Müller-Fahrenholz's vision and honesty. He is able to hold together guilt, shame and forgiveness in a way that is rare but not unique. Arnold's (1998) *The Lost Art of Forgiveness* tells the moving stories of people who have forgiven. He calls these 'stories of healing from the cancer of bitterness'. Both books demonstrate one of the fundamental problems in the way people often deal with forgiveness. This is that people want to split it off from the rest of their life and try and deal with it at either a psychological or a faith level. Rarely does this work. Such a way of dealing with forgiveness may account for the fact that the issue of forgiveness is a major pastoral problem. In a survey of the kinds of issues taken to ministers in the evangelical tradition, which has a particular focus on forgiveness as a crucial aspect of faith, unforgiveness was one of the top four pastoral problems alongside stress, marriage guidance and bereavement (Francis 2000: 12). Too glibly texts from the Bible have been used, leaving people feeling condemned, because deep down they know that they have not been able to forgive others, or they feel unforgiven themselves. Although the words say that they have been forgiven by God, they are unable to experience this in their relationship with God (Collins 1988b: 144). In a similar vein, psychotherapy has only discussed forgiveness relatively recently. It is remarkably absent from the literature that has devoted much more space to the subject of guilt. Yet it is not without a voice. Anna Freud, talking to a fellow psychoanalyst about a patient, commented,

> But what in the world we would want for her. Oh, I don't mean psychotherapy! She's had lots of that. It would take more years, I suspect, of psychoanalysis than the good Lord has given her . . . This poor old lady doesn't need us at all . . . What she needs . . . is forgiveness. She needs to make peace with her soul, not talk about her mind. There must be a God, somewhere to help her, to hear her, to heal her . . . and we certainly aren't the ones who will be of assistance to her in that regard!
>
> (Quoted in Arnold 1998: 120)

It would seem that the subject of forgiveness challenges theological and faith worlds to find a psychological voice, and the psychotherapeutic and counselling worlds to find a spiritual voice. Atkinson does this in his work on counselling in a theological context where he finds the parallels in psychotherapy through the concept of reparation as developed by Melanie Klein. A child needs to come to terms with the ambiguity that he or she experiences in the most powerful positive and negative emotions felt towards the mother.

> This is what Klein calls the guilt which arises from having felt aggressive to the mother who cares. So there is a desire on the part of the child to make reparation – to make good the injuries the child in fantasy carried out upon its mother. For reparation to happen, the mother needs to 'hold' the child psychologically in time so that this process of making good can proceed ... only if the mother can recognize the 'wrong', and provide a context in which it can be faced, acknowledged, and creatively left behind. When that happens, the child is able to move into the stage of creativity – the 'stage of concern', the capacity to love.
>
> (Bridger and Atkinson 1994: 207)

The nature and extent of forgiveness requires the theological and the therapeutic to work together. How does this happen? There are a number of steps or stages in a process of forgiveness that contain elements of both the theological and the therapeutic. A number of these elements are included in the tasks, skills and relational qualities that have been described in previous chapters. But it is important to note that forgiveness is a hard process, and a long-term process that cannot be rushed. If forgiveness is rushed or guilt and shame are covered over, the wound remains lingering, infected, unhealed and hurting. Forgiveness is not a step-by-step process; more often we discover it by looking back and identifying key landmarks:

> Patton argues that people only retrospectively discover they have forgiven others when they have actually given up the claim to have the ability to do so: 'human forgiveness is not doing something but discovering something – that I am more like those who have hurt me than different from them.

I am able to forgive when I discover that I am in no position to forgive'.

(Pattison 2000: 198)

If there are not identifiable stages, there are nonetheless pointers along the way that leads to forgiveness.

The story needs to be told

I have said it before, and I say it again. Behind every broken relationship, fractured trust and abusive encounter there lies a story. The moment by moment events, the fleeting emotions, the buried anger and rage, the burning shame all need a place in the narrative of forgiveness. Arnold's (1997) *The Lost Art of Forgiving* lets people tell their stories of events that led to their facing forgiveness. The stories are dramatic and the demands made upon the people concerned are immense. There are not always happy endings, but the stories raise the challenging and elusive nature of forgiveness.

> Not all stories have tidy endings. Even when we are able to confront the person we need to forgive, they may not be the least bit sorry for their actions. Sometimes a murderer is never apprehended, or a marriage partner runs away, never to be seen again. Is forgiveness still possible?
>
> (Arnold 1997: 70)

The stories we are likely to hear will probably not have the same dramatic quality as those he narrates – they are not about kidnap, torture and murder – but the pastoral helper is likely to hear stories of abuse, rape, violence, deceit, loss, love and despair. These stories are just as important, and in revealing hurt and bitterness they may also uncover the inability to forgive.

The details need to be heard

Each story has particular moments and particular words that get to the heart of the events. Time and again the wounds people carry are packaged in a form of words that reverberate like some nightmarish echo. Often these words are linked to experiences and feelings of being shamed. The experience of being in counselling is that as words are uttered and reflected back and acknowledged, they take on a three-dimensional shape. They become real in a way that they were not whilst still in a person's thoughts. To use Müller-Fahrenholz's image, the words reveal the inner person just as a mirror reveals the physical person, yet with new depth and colour.

The emotions need to be felt and held

'The counsellor's empathic response may be complex for the client. If the abuser's denial, the collusion of bystanders, injunctions "not to get angry but to forgive", and the abused person's own need to survive conspire to mask the full weight of an experience of abuse, the counsellor's empathy is likely to unmask it' (Layzell 1999: 121). Atkinson suggests that Klein's understanding of people's ability to make reparation as a psychological act of forgiveness demands that the mother, the pastoral carer, or the counsellor 'hold' the person and his or her ambivalent emotions. This holding sounds simpler than it is, and it is a task that in some cases can take years of professional help. But holding the emotions can also bring relief in the briefer contacts of pastoral work, where it is the depth of the acceptance and empathy that are equally important.

An encounter with the Other

Just as it is often a broken relationship that brings about the need for forgiveness, it is through relationship with another person that strength, acceptance and a resource for forgiveness becomes possible. It is not always possible to mend relationships that have broken: 'Apologies are not always forthcoming; and it is sometimes impossible to feel compassion for the wrongdoer. Here, we must turn to the possibility that God's compassion is not limited, relieving the injured party from having to shoulder the task of forgiveness alone' (Watts *et al.* 2002: 30). Expressed in Christian thought, 'The tender heart of God is broken open on the Cross, expressing the lengths God in forgiving love is prepared to go so that relationships might be restored' (Bridger and Atkinson 1994: 207). Eugene Heimler, a rabbi who survived the Holocaust, found a new encounter with the Torah as his source of help in a long process of reconciliation. 'I was moved to hear my students speaking about Ruah – spirit – or about Yexer Harah – the evil inclination – or Yezer Tov – the good inclination. I have felt the absolute necessity not simply to talk about the Holocaust but rather to do' (1988: 99ff.).

An act of choosing

In choosing forgiveness as an option we have the possibility of becoming free. 'Forgiveness seems to release us from those who hurt us, while resentment and vengeance binds us to those whom we cannot forgive' (Watts *et al.* 2002: 30). Yet it is not a comfortable choice and neither is it an irrevocable step. 'Such a step involves surrendering control and choosing to live with insecurity, vulnerability and risk. It means relinquishing the desire for vengeance in order to forgive, replacing hate with love, living hopefully and generously, by faith and trust' (Layzell 1999: 122). It is always possible to step back into a place of unforgiveness, when the pain and hurt are reawoken by an unexpected event (Ross 1997). The week by week liturgical recalling of forgiveness in the prayers of different faiths is a resource that suggests that forgiveness is an ongoing commitment.

This chapter has touched on huge and complex themes of guilt, shame and forgiveness – showing that a vital part of our tangled humanity is expressed through our faith and psychological functioning. It offers no easy answers and focuses yet again on the importance of the pastoral relationship. The more such a relationship can acknowledge and locate guilt and shame, without repeating the negative aspects of these experiences, the greater healing a person can encounter. That healing may or may not include the experience of forgiveness, but can valuably sustain the person and his or her faith while this process comes about.

Conclusion

As I was writing the conclusion to this book the telephone rang. When I answered it the person speaking launched into a jumbled description of marriage difficulties and her current depression before abruptly saying 'I'm looking for Christian counselling. Are you a Christian counsellor?' Such a conversation underlined for me why I was writing this book in the first place – to help people struggling with faith, life and all its problems. My aim has been to equip the reader to offer pastoral care, aided by counselling skills, in a professional way. This book presents a model of pastoral skills based on different counselling theories including psychodynamic, person-centred and narrative approaches. The first eleven chapters have developed this model with its three distinct phases, outlining the specific tasks, skills and relational qualities that are required. It has drawn primarily from Christian and Jewish perspectives, though it touches on aspects of all religious traditions. The last three chapters, covering important and difficult subjects, demonstrate that it is possible to use this counselling skills model in a variety of complex situations.

Yet the theme that resonates with me is not so much what we 'do' to people, as is possible with such a counselling skills model, but how we 'are' with people. My hope is that readers will be wiser people because they have encountered new ideas or familiar concepts, applied in a relevant way. Another part of this hope is that readers will have been touched by the brief lives spoken of in these pages, whose very struggles so often reflect our own. This hope goes deeper, in that part of me desires that readers will have encountered their own being, that elusive 'true self', perhaps only fully known to God, which is at the heart of what one person offers to another. This hope also has a vital spiritual dimension in that it is as we encounter our self and others that there can be a renewed encounter with our faith traditions and our personal faith in God.

Endings are always difficult, even when writing a book. What are the things that we are not brave enough to say until the very end, and even then courage sometimes fails us? Endings are about loss and love. For me these are the two central themes at the heart of faith, counselling and psychotherapy. This book, then, marks an end of a journey that encounters loss and love in equal measure, that I hope will help others on their own journey of bringing help and healing to others.

References

Arnold, J. (1998) *The Lost Art of Forgiveness*. Robertsbridge: Plough Publishing.

Atkinson, D. (1995) Guilt, in D. Atkinson and D. Field (eds) *New Dictionary of Pastoral Theology and Christian Ethics*. Leicester: IVP.

Baptist Union (2002) Safe to Grow. Oxford: Baptist Union.

Bartholemew, C. (2002) Seizing the day, *Word In Action*, Spring. Swindon: Bible Society.

Bateman, A. and Holmes, J. (1995) *Introduction to Psychoanalysis*. London: Routledge.

Beck, J. (1999) Doubt, in D. Benner and C. Hill (eds) *Baker Encyclopedia of Psychology and Counselling*, 2nd edn. Grand Rapids, MI: Baker Books.

Beit-Hallahmi, B. and Argyle, M. (1997) *The Psychology of Religious Behaviour, Belief and Experience*. London: Routledge.

Bettelheim, B. (1979) *Surviving and Other Essays*. New York, NY: Vintage Books.

Bomford, R. (1999) *The Symmetry of God*. London: Free Association Books.

Bond, T. (1993) *Standards and Ethics for Counselling in Action*. London: Sage Publications.

Bowlby, J. (1988) *A Secure Base*. London: Routledge.

Boyd, A. and Lynch, G. (1999) Establishing the therapeutic frame in pastoral settings, in G. Lynch (ed.) *Clinical Counselling in Pastoral Settings*. London: Routledge.

Brayer, M. (1990) Sexuality, Jewish theology and ethics of, in R. Hunter (ed.) *Dictionary of Pastoral Care and Counselling*. Nashville, TN: Abingdon.

Bridger, F. and Atkinson, D. (1994) *Counselling in Context*. London: HarperCollins.

British Association for Counselling and Psychotherapy (BACP) (1998) *Invitation to Membership*. Rugby: BACP.

British Association for Counselling and Psychotherapy (BACP) (2002) *Ethical Framework for Good Practice in Counselling and Psychotherapy*. Rugby: BACP.

Burns, P. (2002) Inside out, *Coracle*, February.

Butler, S. (1999) *Caring Ministry*. New York, NY: Continuum.

Campbell, A. (1986) *Rediscovering Pastoral Care*, 2nd edn. London: DLT.

Clarkson, P. (1995) *The Therapeutic Relationship*. London: Whurr.

Coate, M. A. (1989) *Clergy Stress*. London: SPCK.

Collins, G. (1988a) *Can You Trust Counselling?* Leicester: IVP.

Collins, G. (1988b) *Christian Counselling*. London: Word.

Coltart, N. (1993) *How to Survive as a Psychotherapist*. London: Sheldon Press.

Coltart, N. (1996) *The Baby and the Bathwater*. London: Karnac Books.

Corey, G. (1996) *Theory and Practice of Counselling and Psychotherapy*, 5th edn. Pacific Grove, CA: Brookes/Cole Publishing.

Cotter, J. (1993) *Pleasure, Pain and Passion*, 2nd edn. Sheffield: Cairns Publications.

Culley, S. (1991) *Integrative Counselling Skills in Action*. London: Sage.

CWR (1996) *Learning to Care*. Farnham: CWR.

Deshpande, L. (2001) *Singled Out or One in the Body?* Cambridge: Grove Books.

Douglas, T. (1995) *Scapegoats*. London: Routledge.

Draucker, C. (1992) *Counselling Survivors of Childhood Sexual Abuse*. London: Sage.

Egan, G. (1994) *The Skilled Helper*, 5th edn. Pacific Grove: Brookes Cole.

Fiddes, P. (1988) *The Creative Suffering of God*. Oxford: Oxford University Press.

Ford, M. (1999) *Wounded Prophet*. London: DLT.

Francis, L. (2000) *Pastoral Care Today*. Farnham: CWR.

Gomez, L. (1997) *An Introduction to Object Relations*. London: Free Association Books.

Goodliff, P. (1998) *Care in a Confused Climate*. London: Darton, Longman & Todd.

Gordon, H. (2000) Guilt: why is it such a burden? *Bishop John Robinson Fellowship Newsletter*, Issue 9, February/March.

Hallett, M. (1997) *Sexual Identity and Freedom in Discipleship*. Cambridge: Grove Books.

Hay, D. (2001) *Word in Action*. Swindon: Bible Society.

Heimler, E. (1988) My memories are alive but my hate has gone, in H. Copper (ed.) *Soul Searching*. London: SCM Press.

Hetherington, A. (1998) The use and abuse of touch in therapy and counselling, *Counselling Psychology Quarterly*, 11: 361–4.

Hetherington, A. (2000a) Exploitation in therapy and counselling: a breach of professional standards, *British Journal of Counselling & Guidance*, 28: 11–22.

Hetherington, A. (2000b) A psychodynamic profile of therapists who sexually exploit their clients, *British Journal of Psychotherapy*, 16: 274–86.

Hetherington, A. (2001) *The Use of Counselling Skills in the Emergency Services*. Buckingham: Open University Press.

Hobson, R. (1985) *Forms of Feeling*. London: Routledge.

Holmes, J. (1993) *John Bowlby and Attachment Theory*. London: Routledge.

Hookway, C. (1995) Doubt, in E. Honderich (ed.) *The Oxford Companion to Philosophy*. Oxford: Oxford University Press.

Hughes, G. (1996) *God of Surprises*, 2nd edn. London: DLT.

Hunter, R. (ed.) (1990) *Dictionary of Pastoral Care and Counselling*. Nashville, TN: Abingdon.

Hurding, R. (1998) *Pathways to Wholeness*. London: Hodder & Stoughton.

Jacobs, M. (1988) *Psychodynamic Counselling in Action*. London: Sage Publications.

Jacobs, M. (1993a) *Still Small Voice*, 2nd edn. London: SPCK.

Jacobs, M. (1993b) *Living Illusions: A Psychology of Belief*. London: SPCK.

Jacobs, M. (ed.) (1995a) *The Care Guide*. London: Cassell.

Jacobs, M. (1995b) *D.W. Winnicott*. London: Sage.

Jacobs, M. (1998) *The Presenting Past*, 2nd edn. Buckingham: Open University Press.

Jacobs, M. (2000) *Swift to Hear*, 2nd edn. London: SPCK.

Jung, C. ([1967] 1995) *Memories, Dreams and Reflections*. London: Collins/Fontana.

Katz, R. (1985) *Pastoral Care and the Jewish Tradition*. Philadelphia, PA: Fortress Press.

Kirk, M. and Leary, T. (1994) *Holy Matrimoney?* Oxford: Lynx.

Kubler-Ross, E. (1970) *On Death and Dying*. New York, NY: Macmillan.

Kogan, I. (1995) *The Cry of Mute Children*. London: Free Association Books.

Kornfeld, M. (1998) *Cultivating Wholeness*. New York, NY: Continuum.

Lago, C. and Thompson, J. (1996) *Race, Culture and Counselling*. Buckingham: Open University Press.

Layzell, R. (1999) Pastoral counselling with those who have experienced abuse in religious settings, in G. Lynch (ed.) *Clinical Counselling in Pastoral Settings*. London: Routledge.

Linley, P. A. and Joseph, S. (2002) Posttraumatic growth, *Counselling*, 13: 14–17.

Lomas, P. (1993) *Cultivating Intuition*. Northvale, NJ: Jason Aronson.

Lomas, P. (1999) *Doing Good?* Oxford: Oxford University Press.

Long, A. (1997) Loss: the journey to rediscovery, *Counselling*, 8: 13–14.

Lyall, D. (1995) *Counselling in the Pastoral and Spiritual Context*. Buckingham: Open University Press.

Lyall, D. (1999) Pastoral counselling in a postmodern context, in G. Lynch (ed.) *Clinical Counselling in Pastoral Settings*. London: Routledge.

Lyall, D. (2001) *The Integrity of Pastoral Care*. London: SPCK.

Lynch, G. (1999) *Clinical Counselling in Pastoral Settings*. London: Routledge.

McGrath, A. (1996) *A Passion for Truth*. Leicester: IVP.

McLemore, C. (1990) Defense mechanisms, in R. Hunter (ed.) *Dictionary of Pastoral Care and Counselling*. Nashville, TN: Abingdon.

McLeod, J. (1997) *Narrative and Psychotherapy*. London: Sage Publications.

McLeod, J. (1998) *Introduction to Counselling*, 2nd edn. Buckingham: Open University Press.

McLoughlin, B. (1995) *Developing Psychodynamic Counselling*. London: Sage Publications.

Magonet, J. (1988) Religious tensions in counselling, in H. Cooper (ed.) *Soul Searching*. London: SCM Press.

Malan, D. (1995) *Individual Psychotherapy*, 2nd edn. Oxford: Butterworth-Heinemann.

Mearns, D. and Thorne, B. (1988) *Person-Centred Counselling in Action*. London: Sage Publications.

Mearns, D. and Thorne, B. (2000) *Person-Centred Therapy Today*. London: Sage Publications.

Merton, T. (1973) *Contemplative Prayer*. London: DLT.

Migliore, D. (1991) *Faith Seeking Understanding*. Grand Rapids, MI: Eerdmans.

Mollon, P. (1996) *Multiple Selves, Multiple Voices*. Chichester: Wiley.

Moltmann, J. (1994) *Jesus Christ for Today's World*. London: SCM Press.

Morley, J. (1992) *All Desires Known*. London: SPCK.

Müller-Fahrenholz, G. (1997) *The Art of Forgiveness*. Geneva: WCC.

Murray-Parkes, C. (1986) *Bereavement: Studies of Grief in Adult Life*. Harmondsworth: Penguin.

Narramore, B. (1984) *No Condemnation*. Grand Rapids, MI: Zondervan.

Nouwen, H. (1992) *The Return of the Prodigal Son*. London: DLT.

Nouwen, H. ([1979] 1994) *The Wounded Healer*. New York: Doubleday.

Oates, W. (1990) Antisocial persons, in R. Hunter (ed.) *Dictionary of Pastoral Care and Counselling*. Nashville, TN: Abingdon.

Oden, T. (1978) *Kerygma and Counselling*. San Francisco, CA: Harper & Row.

Oden, T. (1983) *Pastoral Theology*. San Francisco, CA: Harper & Row.

Oden, T. (1984) *Care of Souls in the Classic Tradition*. Philadelphia, PA: Fortress Press.

Orbach, S. (1994) *What's Really Going In Here?* London: Virago.

Orbach, S. (1999) *The Impossibility of Sex*. London: Allen Lane.

Pattison, E. (1990) Defense and coping theory, in R. Hunter (ed.) *Dictionary of Pastoral Care and Counselling*. Nashville, TN: Abingdon.

Pattison, S. (2000) *Shame*. Cambridge: Cambridge University Press.

Patton, M. and Meara, N. (1992) *Psychoanalytic Counselling*. Chichester: Wiley.

Perry, C. (1991) *Listen to the Voice Within*. London: SPCK.

Peters, T. (1994) *Sin – Radical Evil in Soul and Society*. Grand Rapids, MI: Eerdmans.

Pierson, L. (1989) *No-Gay Areas*. Nottingham: Grove Books.

Pokorny, M. (1988) The survivor syndrome, in H. Copper (ed.) *Soul Searching*. London: SCM Press.

Pruyser, P. (1990) Doubt and unbelief, in R. Hunter (ed.) *Dictionary of Pastoral Care and Counselling*. Nashville, TN: Abingdon.

Rayburn, C. (1999) Power, in D. Benner and C. Hill (eds) *Baker Encyclopedia of Psychology and Counselling*, 2nd edn. Grand Rapids, MI: Baker Books.

Rayner, E. (1986) *Human Development*, 3rd edn. London: Unwin Hyman.

Ricoeur, P. (1970) *Freud and Philosophy*. New Haven, CT: Yale University Press.

Rodman, F. R. (1987) *The Spontaneous Gesture*. London: Karnac.

Rogers, C. (1980) *A Way of Being*. Boston, MA: Houghton Mifflin.

Rogers, E. (1999) *Sexuality and the Christian Body*. Oxford: Blackwell.

Ross, J. A. (1997) *Evangelicals in Exile: Wrestling with Theology and the Unconscious*. London: DLT.

Ross, J. A. (1999) Religious tradition in pastoral counselling, in G. Lynch (ed.) *Clinical Counselling in Pastoral Settings*. London: Routledge.

Ross, J. A. (2001) Learning to Listen, *Third Way*, 24: 23–6.

Rowan, J. (1983) *The Reality Game*. London: Routledge.

Sacks, J. (1995) *Faith in the Future*. London: Darton, Longman & Todd.

Sanderson, C. (1995) *Counselling Adult Survivors of Child Sexual Abuse*, 3rd edn. London: Jessica Kingsley.

Schneider, C. (1990) Shame, in R. Hunter (ed.) *Dictionary of Pastoral Care and Counselling*. Nashville, TN: Abingdon.

Small, R. and Lumley, J. (2001) Psychological debriefing: providing good clinical care means listening to women's concerns, *British Medical Journal*, 322: 928.

Smith, R. (1966) *Martin Buber*. London: Carey Kingsgate Press.

Sperry, L. (2001) *Spirituality in Clinical Practice*. Hove: Brunner Routledge.

Stein, E. (1990) Guilt, in R. Hunter (ed.) *Dictionary of Pastoral Care and Counselling*. Nashville, TN: Abingdon.

Stevens, J. (1971) *Awareness*. Moab, UT: Real People Press.

Stroup, G. (1981) *The Promise of Narrative Theology*. London: SCM.

Strozier, C. (1997) Heinz Kohut's struggles with religion, ethnicity, and God, in J. Jacobs and D. Capps (eds) *Religion, Society and Psychoanalysis*. Oxford: Westview Press.

Thomas, J. (1987) Doubt, in A. Campbell (ed.) *Dictionary of Pastoral Care*. London: SPCK.

Thorne, B. (1998) *Person-centred Counselling and Christian Spirituality*. London: Whurr Publishers.

Tidball, D. (1988) Doubt, in S. Ferguson, D. Wright and J. Packer (eds) *New Dictionary of Theology*. Leicester: IVP.

Townsend, C. (1994) Homosexuality: finding the way of truth and love, *Cambridge Papers*, 3: 2.

Trower, P., Casey, A. and Dryden, W. (1988) *Cognitive Behavioural Counselling in Action*. London: Sage Publications.

Truax, C. and Carkhuff, R. (1967) *Towards Effective Counselling and Psychotherapy*. Chicago, IL: Aldine.

Vanhoozer, K. (1990) *Biblical Narrative in the Philosophy of Paul Ricoeur*. Cambridge: Cambridge University Press.

Vasey, M. (1991) *Evangelical Christians and Gay Rights*. Nottingham: Grove Books.

Virgo, L. (1987) *First Aid in Pastoral Care*. Edinburgh: T&T Clark.

Walker, M. (1992) *Surviving Secrets*. Buckingham: Open University Press.

Walker, M. (ed.) (1999) *Hidden Selves*. Buckingham: Open University Press.

Ward, I. (1993) *Is Psychoanalysis Another Religion?* London: Freud Museum.

Watts, F., Nye, R. and Savage, S. (2002) *Psychology for Christian Ministry*. London: Routledge.

Webster, J. (1993) Faith, in A. McGrath (ed.) *Modern Christian Thought*. Oxford: Blackwell.

Whitmore, D. (2000) *Psychosynthesis Counselling in Action*, 2nd edn. London: Sage Publications.

Winnicott, D. (1986) *Home Is Where We Start From*. Harmondsworth: Penguin.

Winnicott, D. (1990) *The Maturational Process and the Facilitating Environment*. London: Karnac.

Worden, W. (1991) *Grief Counselling and Grief Therapy*, 2nd edn. London: Routledge.

Wright, K. (1991) *Vision and Separation*. Northvale: Jason Aronson.
Wright, N. (2002) *The Bible in Transmission*. Swindon: Bible Society.
Yalom, I. (1989) *Love's Executioner*. Harmondsworth: Penguin Books.
Yancey, P. (1995) *Disappointment with God*. London: HarperCollins.

Index